Explaining Bipolar Disorder

Doreen Jarrett

Emerald Guides
www.emeraldpublishing.co.uk

Emerald Guides

British Cataloguing in Publication Data. A catalogue record is available for this book from the British library.

ISBN
978-1-84716-413-1

Printed by Grosvenor Group London

Cover design by Bookworks Islington

Contents

Ch 1. Introduction 11

What is Bi-polar Disorder? 11
Signs and symptoms of bipolar disorder 11
Manic episodes 12
Hypomania 13
Depression 13
Signs and symptoms of a mixed episode 14
Different types of bipolar disorder 14
Length and frequency of episodes 15
What causes bipolar disorder? 15
Childhood distress 16
General problems in life 16
Childhood bipolar disorder 17
Implications for pregnancy and childbirth 19
Main points from chapter one 23

Ch 2 Bi-polar Disorder-Support and Self-help-Taking 25
Control of Your Situation

Living with bipolar disorder-what you can do to help 25
yourself
Know your early warning signs 27
Putting together a personal self-help pack 27
Create an emergency action plan 28
Develop a daily routine 29
Stress 30
Diet 30
Main points from chapter 2 32

Ch 3. Treatment for Bi-polar Disorder-Medication   35

NICE guidance   35
learning about medication   36
Types of medication   37
Lithium   37
Anticonvulsant drugs   38
Anti-depressants   38
Ant-psychotic drugs   41
Anti-parkinsonian drugs   42
Medications and pregnancy   42
Main points from chapter 3   44

Ch 4. Professional Help and Support   45

Young people and bipolar   45
General practitioners-the first stop   45
What you can do   46
What to expect from your doctor   48
Community mental health teams   48
Psychotherapy   49
Psychodynamic therapists   50
Care-coordinators   50
Hospitalisation   51
Main points from chapter 4   52

Ch 5. More about behavioural therapies   53

What is cognitive behavioural therapy?   53
Cognitive therapy   53
Behavioural therapy   54
Cognitive behavioural therapy   54

How can I get cognitive behavioural therapy? 57
Do-it-yourself cognitive behavioural therapy 58
Main points from chapter 5 59

Ch 6. Dealing With Stigma and Shame 61

Bipolar-stigmatisation and feelings of shame 61
Stigma 61
Effects of stigma 62
Main points from chapter 6 66

Ch 7. Bipolar Disorder and Vicious Cycles 67

Vicious cycles and stress 68
Relaxation 68
Breathing exercise 69
Progressive muscle relaxation 70
Visualisation 71
Controlling anger 72
Understanding your anger pattern 73
Suppressing anger 73
Main points from chapter 7 76

Ch 8. Assertiveness-the Importance of Being Assertive 77
in the Control of Vicious Cycles

Non-assertiveness 77
Non-assertive body language 78
Assertiveness 78
Assertive body language 78
Aggressiveness 79
Aggressive body language 79
How to improve the communication process 79

Assertive ways of saying no   79
Main points from chapter 8   81

Ch 9. The Risks of Sleep Loss   83

How bipolar disorder affects sleep   83
Getting better sleep with bipolar disorder   84
Main points from chapter 9   89

Ch 10. Bipolar Disorder-Family Issues   91

Involvement of spouses and partners   92
Family breakdown and rebuilding relationships   93
Main points from chapter 10   95

Ch 11. Bipolar disorder and diet   97

Is there a specific diet for bipolar disorder?   97
Does fish oil improve mood?   98
Which foods to avoid   99
What about alcohol and bipolar disorder?   100
Grapefruit juice   101
Medication and food   102
Main points from chapter 10   103

Ch 12. Rights in the workplace   105

Rights of the employee   105
Working with bipolar   105
Warning signs at work   106
Examples of different warning signs   106
Medication   107
Self-management   107

Support   108
The Health and Safety at Work Act 1974   108
The Disability Discrimination Act 1995 as amended 108
  Unlawful discrimination in employment   109
  The Equality Act 2010   110
  Return to Work   111
  Access to Work `````   111
  Main points from chapter 12   112

Chapter 13. Welfare Benefits and Bipolar Disorder   113

  The range of welfare benefits available   113
  Checking your benefit entitlement   113
  Universal credit   114
  Employment and support allowance   114
  Job seekers allowance   116
  Income support   117
  Incapacity benefit   117
  Severe disablement allowance   118
  Statutory sick pay   118
  Working tax credit   119
  Disability living allowance/ personal independence
  payment (PIP)   120
  Housing benefit   121
  Local Housing Allowance   123
  Support for mortgage interest   124
  Council tax support and discounts   125
  The Social fund   127
  Main points from chapter 13   129

Conclusion
Useful addresses and websites
Index

1

Introduction

This book is intended to provide a comprehensive overview of the condition known as bipolar disorder. The book aims to be of use to those who have the condition and also family and friends who are affected by the condition.

What is bipolar disorder?

Bipolar disorder is the term used to describe what was once known as manic depression. Bipolar disorder causes serious shifts in mood, energy, thinking and behaviour.

Essentially, if you have bipolar disorder you will experience extreme swings in mood-from periods of hyperactivity, known as 'mania' or 'manic episodes' to deep depression. Some people also see or hear things around them that others don't (known as visual or auditory hallucinations) or have uncommon, unshared beliefs (known as delusions). In periods of calm, usually through some form of medication, you will find yourself 'level' and behaving normally.

Signs and symptoms of bi-polar disorder

There are four types of mood episode in bipolar disorder: mania, hypomania, depression and mixed episodes.

Manic episodes

In the manic phase of bipolar disorder, feelings of heightened energy, creativity, and euphoria are common. People experiencing a manic episode often talk very fast, sleep very little and are hyperactive Such a person may feel that they are all-powerful, invincible or destined for greatness.

To summarise, symptoms might include:

- A feeling of euphoria
- Feelings of restlessness
- Extreme irritability
- Talking very fast
- Racing thoughts
- lack of concentration
- Lots of energy
- A reduced need for sleep
- A sense of own importance
- Poor judgement
- Excessive and inappropriate spending
- Increased sexual drive
- Risky behaviour
- Misuse of drugs or alcohol
- Aggressive behaviour

While mania might feel good in the first instance, it has a tendency to spiral out of control. The aggressive side of mania can be a particular problem, picking fights, lashing out and so on.

Hypomania

Hypomania is a less severe form of mania. people in a hypomanic state feel euphoric, energetic and productive, but they are able to carry on with their day-to-day lives and they never lose touch with reality. To others, it may seem that people with hypomania are in an unusually good mood. However, hypomania can result in bad decisions that can harm relationships with others and also harm careers and reputations. In addition, hypomania can also escalate to a full-blown mania.

Depression

In the past, bipolar depression was seen as general depression. Doctors couldn't differentiate. However, a growing body of research suggests that there is a significant difference between the two, especially when it comes to recommended treatments. Whereas doctors tend to prescribe anti-depressants in many cases, these will not always help those with bipolar disorder. In fact, it has been proved that they can make the condition worse, triggering mania.

Despite many similarities, certain symptoms are more common in bipolar depression than in regular depression. For example, bipolar depression is more likely to involve irritability, guilt, unpredictable mood swings and restlessness. People with bipolar depression also tend to move and speak slowly, sleep a lot and gain weight. In addition, they are more likely to develop psychotic depression-a condition where a person loses contact with reality and also to experience major problems with social functioning, which can affect work. Common symptoms of bipolar depression include:

- Feeling hopeless, sad or empty
- Irritability
- Inability to experience pleasure
- Fatigue or loss of energy
- Physical or mental sluggishness
- Appetite or weight changes
- Sleep problems
- Concentration and memory problems
- Feelings of worthlessness or guilt
- Thoughts of death or suicide

Signs and symptoms of a mixed episode

A mixed episode of bipolar disorder, as its name suggests, is where a person will exhibit symptoms of both mania, hypomania and depression. Common signs of a mixed episode include depression combined with agitation, irritability, anxiety, distractibility and racing thoughts. This combination of moods makes for a very high risk of suicide.

Different types of bipolar disorder

Bipolar disorder is further categorized as:

- Bipolar 1 disorder, which is mania or mixed episode. This is the classic manic-depressive form of the illness, characterized by at least one manic or mixed episode. Usually, but not in all cases, bipolar 1 will involve at least one episode of depression.
- Bipolar 2 disorder (hypomania and depression). In bipolar 2 disorder the person doesn't experience full

blown manic episodes. Instead the illness involves a mixture of hypomania and severe depression.

- Cyclothymia (hypermania and mild depression). Cyclothymia is a milder form of bipolar disorder. It consists of cyclical mood swings. However, the symptoms are less severe than full-blown mania or depression.

Length and frequency of episodes

A person may have very few bipolar disorder episodes, with years of stability in between each episode. However, they may also experience many more. Episodes can vary in length and frequency from weeks to months, with varying lengths of time in between.

Mania usually starts suddenly and lasts between two weeks and four to five months. Depression often lasts longer, on average around six months, but can last longer, but usually less than a year.

Although a person may cope very well in between episodes, they may experience low-level symptoms in these relatively 'stable' periods which can impact on daily life.

What causes bipolar disorder?

Like a lot of other conditions, for example, Parkinson's, very little is known about the sources of bipolar disorder. However, it does run in families, which suggests a genetic link. On the other hand, there may not be a family link and the origin may lie elsewhere. This is one of the problems with diagnosing the causes of bipolar disorder. Unless the link is obvious then the origins remain obscure. The disorder is diagnosed in a roughly equal number of men or women. It usually starts in the 20's and 30's, although it can also start as a teenager.

The fact that symptoms can be controlled by medication, especially lithium and anticonvulsants (see chapter 3) suggests that there may be problems with the functions of the nerves in the brain. This is supported by research. Disturbances in the endocrine system (controlling hormones) may also be involved.

Most research suggests that a stressful environment, social factors, or physical illness may trigger the condition. Although stress is unlikely to cause bipolar disorder, it seems to be a significant trigger. A person may find that the start of bipolar episodes can be linked to a period of great stress, such as childbirth, a relationship breakdown, money problems or a career change. Sleep disturbance can be an important contributor.

Childhood distress

Some experts believe that a person may develop bipolar disorder if they experienced severe emotional damage in early life, such as physical, sexual or emotional abuse. Grief, loss trauma and neglect can be contributory factors-they can shock the developing mind and produce unbearable stress.

General problems in life

It is also very possible that bipolar disorder can be a reaction to overwhelming problems in day-to-day life. Mania can be a way of escaping unbearable depression. For example, if a person appears to have very over-inflated sense of one's own self-importance and

Bi-Polar disorder-implications for pregnancy and childbirth

For any women (and man) having a baby is a major event and quite often a stressful time Women with bipolar disorder, and their families and friends, will have numerous questions to which they will need answers. Common questions might be:

- Will the birth of the baby affect me in any way, will I become ill?
- Is bipolar hereditary-will my children develop bipolar disorder?
- Will my medication affect my pregnancy and my baby?

Firstly, each woman's experience is unique, therefore it is difficult to give general answers to questions that will apply to all women.

Discussing pregnancy with your GP and psychiatric team

It is best to discuss issues surrounding pregnancy before you even start to try for a baby. Some GP's and psychiatrists have a special interest in psychiatric illness and childbirth, which is sometimes called Perinatal psychiatry. Not all areas in the UK are covered by Perinatal teams. If you are fortunate enough to live in an area where there is a team, then you can be referred to them. If there is no local service then you may have to travel.

A few questions answered
1. Risks of becoming ill during pregnancy and after childbirth
Women with bipolar disorder may become unwell during pregnancy but are at a particularly high risk of becoming ill following childbirth. There is a risk of severe manic and

depressive episodes. In addition, mood symptoms such as elation, irritability and depression can occur, along with psychotic symptoms such as delusions and hallucinations. When such symptoms are severe it may be called an episode pf postpartum psychosis or puerperal psychosis. Other mood episodes at this time may be labelled as 'postnatal depression' or 'postpartum depression'. Women who experience severe episodes following pregnancy may require hospitalisation but usually respond well to treatment.

Two groups of women with bipolar disorder are at higher risk: those who have had a previous period of severe illness following childbirth, and those with a relative who has suffered postpartum psychosis. Women with bipolar disorder must think very carefully about these risks before becoming pregnant.

2. What can I do to lower the risks of becoming ill?

The main thing here is to ensure that you let all those involved know that you have bipolar disorder and that there is a real risk of becoming unwell again after childbirth. Your midwife, GP, health visitor and obstetrician should all be made aware of your bipolar and of your past history. Anyone else who is involved with you such as your CPN or psychiatrist should also be told. As discussed above, you should inform everyone who is relevant before you become pregnant.

Paying attention to other issues known to increase the risk of becoming ill may be important. These include trying to reduce other stressful things going on in your life. paying attention to sleep, before and after your baby is born is important. With a new baby, this can be difficult but you will need as much support as possible from your partner.

3. Will my children contact bi-polar disorder?

It is a fact that many illnesses run in families. This is true for all sorts of conditions, such as diabetes, heart conditions and cancer, but also for psychiatric disorders. However, although the children of people with bipolar disorder may be at a higher risk of becoming ill than people in general it is by no means a foregone conclusion. Only about 10% of children who have a parent with illness develop it themselves, so the majority are likely to stay well.

4. Will my medication affect my pregnancy?

On the whole, most medications present a low risk. However, it is necessary to discuss this with your GP who will have a better idea of any side effects of a particular drug. One thing is certain, stopping medication suddenly can increase the risks of illness.

5. Will my condition affect breastfeeding?

Whilst it is possible to breastfeed while taking some medications, you need to be fully aware of the risks involved. It may be that you are unable to breastfeed. There are several reasons why this is the case. You may be too unwell or you may be admitted to hospital without your baby. You may need a medication which is not safe in breastfeeding. Additionally, getting up in the night to breastfeed may cause sleep deprivation, or exacerbate the sleep deprivation that you are already experiencing which poses a risk to you.

6. What sort of care will I receive during pregnancy?

If you have bipolar disorder it is important that you receive specialist care during pregnancy. If Perinatal treatment is available in your area you should see the team, if not you should see a psychiatrist. The outcome should be a written care plan for you. Your midwives will also offer support during this period.

When you go home after you have had your baby, your mental health should be closely monitored. Your midwife, health visitor and mental health nurse should visit regularly in the first few weeks after your baby is born. If you become unwell during this period this can be picked up quickly so you can get early treatment.

In the next chapter, we will look at what you can do to help yourself if you have been diagnosed with bipolar disorder. Having understood something about the nature of bipolar disorder by reading this chapter, it is now time to understand what you can do to ensure that you can at least have as normal a life as possible.

Now read the main points from chapter one overleaf.

****

Main points from Chapter One

❖ Bipolar disorder is the term used to describe what was once known as manic depression. Bipolar disorder causes serious shifts in mood, energy, thinking and behaviour.

❖ There are four types of mood episode in bipolar disorder: mania, hypomania, depression and mixed episodes.

❖ Like a lot of other conditions, for example, Parkinson's, very little is known about the sources of bipolar disorder. However, it does run in families, which suggests a genetic link. On the other hand, there may not be a family link and the origin may lie elsewhere.

❖ Childhood bipolar disorder, also known as pediatric bipolar disorder, is a form of bipolar disorder that occurs, as its name suggests, in children. While its existence is still a matter of some academic debate and disagreement, there is a growing body of evidence that suggests that bipolar disorder can exist in children.

❖ Bipolar disorder can affect women who are pregnant and also have implications after child birth. It is highly advisable to consult your GP and mental health team about issues surrounding pregnancy.

2

Bipolar Disorder-Support and Self-Help-Taking Control of Your Situation

In chapters 3 and 4, we will be looking at medication and other treatments available to help you control your condition. However, before we describe these there are some general tips that are essential to ensure that you stay in control of your day-to-day life and don't let bipolar disorder control you. Everything that we discuss here will be discussed in more depth as we progress through the book.

Living with bipolar disorder-what you can do to help yourself

If you want to live a decent life with bipolar disorder, and not let it control you, you need to control the condition. This principle applies to many conditions that affect the way people interact on a day-to-day basis. It is very important that you make right and healthy choices for yourself. Doing so will minimise mood episodes, or minimise the effects of these on you and others.

Managing bipolar disorder starts with proper treatment, including medication and therapy. However, there is so much more that you can do to help yourself on a day-to-day basis. The medical profession and other professions that have involvement with you can only go so far. The rest is up to you.

There are key recovery concepts that are fundamental to self-help in managing bipolar disorder:

- *Self-belief, faith in yourself and hope.* With effective symptom management it is very possible to experience prolonged periods of wellness. Believing that you can cope with your mood disorder is essential to future recovery. This is the main tenet, belief, hope and faith in yourself. I have known people who revert to drink out of a sense of hopelessness which is exactly the wrong thing to do. Don't revert to drink, revert to your own inner strength.

- *Taking responsibility.* This follows on from the first principle. It is up to you to take action to keep your moods stabilised. This includes asking help from others when needed, not keeping yourself buttoned up, too proud to open up. Take your medication as prescribed and keep appointments with health care providers.

- *Self- advocacy.* This means being assertive and ensuring that you get the best treatment and support for yourself. In the end, it is you as an individual that is affected and you must represent yourself. Open up to professionals and make sure that they are providing you with the best service.

- *Educate yourself.* Make sure that you understand everything about your condition. Only when you are enlightened can you make sure that you know what you want and how to get it.

- *Finally, support.* Support from others is essential to maintain your stability and enhance your quality of life. Support means from family, friends and professionals.

Know your early warning signs

It is very important to know the warning signs of an oncoming manic or depressive episode. In order to recognize them, you should have a list of the previous symptoms that preceded earlier episodes. You should try to identify the triggers that have caused the onset of an episode in the past, what the influences were. If they were outside influences, then what were they? Common triggers can be:

- Stress-a very common trigger.
- Arguments with loved ones including family.
- Problems at school or work.
- Lack of sleep.
- Too much alcohol.

What you are trying to achieve here is a form of self-monitoring so you are building up an historical pattern which will aid you in the future. Get to know yourself and put yourself in a position where you can recognize episodes as they happen or are beginning to happen. One way of monitoring your symptoms is by keeping a mood chart. Although this might seem laborious, in fact it can provide valuable information about your emotional state and other symptoms that you are having. It can also include information such as how much sleep you are getting, what your sleep patterns are, your diet and alcohol intake and also your medication and how this is affecting you.

Putting together a personal self-help pack

Building on from the above, if you spot any early warning signs of mania or depression, it is important to act quickly, in order to stay in control. In such times, you need a *self-help pack* to draw from. This consists of actions that you can take at any one given time.

Many people with bipolar disorder have found the following to be helpful in reducing symptoms and maintaining well-being:

- Talk to a supportive person
- Make sure you get a full eight hours sleep
- Cut back on activities
- Attend a support group
- Talk regularly (as possible) to your doctor or therapist
- Ensure that you take time to relax and unwind
- Keep regular notes, as discussed above
- Make sure that you exercise regularly
- Cut back on sugar, alcohol and caffeine
- Increase exposure to light

Create an emergency action plan

As with everything in life, it is always best to have an action plan that you can refer to if you run into trouble. When your own safety is at stake you may have to act quickly. A plan of action should include:

- A list of emergency contacts (doctor, therapist, family members)
- A list of all medications that you are taking, including dosage information
- Information about any other health problems that you have

- Symptoms that indicate that you need others to take responsibility for your care
- Treatments preferences-i.e. a list of medications that do not work-who is authorised to take decisions on your behalf etc.

Having a strong support system is vital to staying happy and stable. Creating a supportive environment includes not only who you choose to surround yourself with but also who to avoid, such as people who drain your energy or leave you feeling negative. Spend time with people who value you and leave you feeling positive about yourself.

Develop a daily routine

Your lifestyle choices will have a significant impact on your moods. These choices include sleeping patterns, eating and exercise patterns and the other many things that you do in your daily life to keep depression at bay.

Build structure into your life. Developing and sticking to a daily schedule can help stabilize the mood swings of bipolar disorder. Include set times for sleeping, eating, socializing, working and relaxing. Try to maintain regular patterns of activity even through emotional ups and downs.

Exercise regularly. Exercise has a beneficial impact on mood and may reduce the number of bipolar episodes that you experience. Aerobic exercise is especially effective at treating depression. Try to incorporate at least 30 minutes of activity at least five times a week into your routine. Walking is also a good choice, for people of all fitness levels.

Keep a strict sleep schedule. Getting too little sleep can trigger mania. It is very important indeed to ensure that you get lots of rest. It is important to get the balance right between too little and too much sleep. The best advice here is to maintain a normal sleep schedule, going to bed at the same time every night and rising at the same time.

Stress

Keep stress to a minimum. Stress can trigger episodes of mania and depression in people with bipolar disorder. Know your limits in life and don't take on too much. Learn how to relax. Relaxation techniques such as deep breathing, yoga, meditation can help improve mood and keep depression at bay.

Make leisure time a priority. Do things for no other reason than it feels good to do them. Switch off, read a book, go away on holiday watch a film. Above all, make sure that this is uninterrupted time to yourself.

Diet and bipolar disorder

From the food you eat to any vitamins that you take, what you put into your body is of vital importance. This applies to everyone, not just those with bi-polar disorder. Eat a healthy diet. For optimal mood eat plenty of fruit and vegetables and whole grains, avoid excessive sugar and also fat intake. Space your meals throughout the day and ensure that your blood sugar doesn't get too low. High carbohydrates can cause mood crashes. Other damaging foods include chocolate, caffeine and processed foods.

Omega 3 fatty acids may decrease mood swings in bi-polar disorder. Omega 3 is available as a nutritional supplement. You can also increase your intake of omega 3 by eating cold-water fish such as salmon, sardines and halibut. Soya beans, pumpkin seeds and walnuts also have a high omega 3 content. We will be expanding on the importance of diet later in the book.

Avoid alcohol and drugs at all costs. Drugs such as marijuana, cocaine, ecstasy and tranquilizers can all trigger depression and affect moods. Even moderate social drinking can upset your balance.

Be cautious when taking medication. Certain prescription and over the counter medications can be problematic for people with bi-polar disorder. Be especially careful with anti-depressant drugs, which can trigger mania. Other drugs that can cause mania include over-the-counter cold medicine, appetite suppressants, caffeine, corticosteroids and thyroid medication.

In the next chapter, we will look at the nature of the different types of medication available to treat bipolar disorder.

Now read the main points from Chapter Two overleaf.

****

Main points from Chapter Two

❖ If you want to live a decent life with bi-polar disorder, and not let it control you, you need to control the condition. This principle applies to many conditions that affect the way people interact on a day-to-day basis. It is very important that you make right and healthy choices for yourself. Doing so will minimise mood episodes, or minimise the effects of these on you and others.

❖ There are key recovery concepts that are fundamental to self-help in managing bi-polar disorder: *Self-belief, faith in your-self and hope, taking responsibility, self-advocacy, educating your-self* and finally, *support from professionals.*

❖ It is very important to know the warning signs of an oncoming manic or depressive episode. In order to recognize them, you should have a list of the previous symptoms that preceded earlier episodes. You should try to identify the triggers that have caused the episode in question.

❖ As with everything in life, it is always best to have an action plan that you can refer to if you run into trouble. When your own safety is at stake you may have to act quickly.

❖ From the food you eat to any vitamins that you take, what you put into your body is of vital importance. Eat a healthy diet. For optimal mood eat plenty of fruit and vegetables and whole grains, avoid excessive sugar and also fat intake. Space your meals throughout the day and ensure that your blood sugar doesn't get too low. High carbohydrates can cause mood crashes.

❖ Be cautious when taking medication

****

3

Treatment for Bipolar Disorder-Initial Diagnosis and Medication

If your GP thinks that you have bi-polar disorder, they may refer you to a psychiatrist. Your psychiatrist or GP should explain all of your options to you and your views should be taken into account before your treatment starts.

NICE Guidance

The National Institute for Health and Care Excellence (NICE) has guidelines for the treatment of bipolar disorder. They suggest that you should be offered structured psychological treatment while you are relatively stable but may be experiencing mild to moderate symptoms.

Usually, the psychological treatment would be given in addition to medication and you should be offered at least 16 sessions. The treatment should cover:

- Education about the illness-including information about the importance of regular daily routine and sleep, and about any medication that you have agreed to take
- How to monitor your mood, detect early warning signs and strategies to prevent symptoms from developing into full-blown episodes
- General coping strategies.

Virtually everyone who has been diagnosed with bipolar disorder will receive medication of one sort or another. Although drugs cannot cure bipolar disorder they help to manage the symptoms. Drugs used include lithium, anticonvulsants and anti-psychotics. It is very important to ensure that you have a full understanding of the medication offered and that you monitor your physical health.

Learning about bi-polar disorder medication

When starting medication for bipolar disorder, you should make sure that you know how to take it safely. Questions that you should ask your doctor include:

- Are there any medical conditions that exacerbate my mood swings? For example, an overactive thyroid gland may mimic the symptoms of bipolar disorder. You should ask your GP to carry out a simple blood test to ascertain this.
- What are the side effects and risks of the medication that is being recommended?
- When and how should the medication be taken?
- Are there any foods or other substances that I should avoid?
- How will the medication interact with my other prescriptions?
- How long will I take this medication for?
- Will withdrawing from the drug be difficult once I start?
- Will my symptoms return once I start taking the medication?

These might seem basic questions and you might expect your GP to answer them as a matter of course. However, this doesn't always happen, so, as explained in the last chapter, make sure that you are in control.

During acute mania or depression you should talk with your doctor at least once a week, or more frequently, to monitor symptoms. As time goes by and you stabilise then you will see your GP less frequently. Once again, it is up to you to see that this happens.

Types of medication
Lithium

Lithium is a mood stabilizer and is the most common form of medication for those with bipolar disorder. It is the most effective medication for treating mania. It can also help depression. However, it is not really effective for mixed episodes. Lithium will take between one to two weeks to take effect.

Lithium is a naturally occurring element, the lightest of the metals and comes as two different salts: Lithium carbonate (Camcolit, Liskonum, Priadel) and Lithium Citrate (Li-Liquid, Priadel). It does not matter which of these that you take, but you should keep to the same one, because they are absorbed slightly differently.

It is very important that lithium is taken at the right level and regular blood tests are essential. It is also very important to drink plenty of fluids every day and alcohol should be taken in moderation as well as coffee and strong tea.

Common side effects of lithium

There are a number of side effects of lithium, both common side effects and more serious. The common side effects are increased thirsts and urination, dry mouth, trembling hands, mild nausea and acne. The more serious side effects are weight gain, excessive urination, thyroid and kidney damage. Toxic effects that can arise as a result of too much lithium in the blood are diarrhoea, intense thirst, persistent nausea and vomiting, confusion, severe tremors and blurred vision. If you are taking lithium and suffer any of these symptoms then it is very important that you have a blood test, as failing to do so can result in kidney damage.

Avoiding toxic lithium levels from developing

There are ways that you can exercise control over the amount of lithium in your blood:

- Make sure that you go for blood tests when they are needed
- Don't suddenly change the amount of salt in your diet
- Make sure that you drink enough fluids
- Control your alcohol intake-keep it to a bare minimum
- See a doctor straight away if you feel that you are developing symptoms relating to toxicity.

Anticonvulsant drugs

Some other drugs are commonly used as mood stabilizers, Sodium valproate and Carbamazepine plus Lamotrigine. Although both were initially used for the management of epilepsy, they have been found to offer benefits to bi-polar patients. Sodium valproate, (common names: Epilim, Divalproex, Depakote) has been found to be effective in patients who suffer predominantly from depression. Common side effects can be: Nausea, vomiting, weight gain, tremors, drowsiness, hair loss.

Carbamazepine, (common name: Tegretolks), works less well in such cases. Common side effects: Dry mouth, nausea, diarrhoea, dizziness, headaches, problems with walking, tiredness and rashes.

Lamotrigine has anti-depressant effects and is licensed for depressive episodes in bipolar disorder. Like lithium anticonvulsants also have to be monitored for excess levels, although not as tightly as lithium. They can also present some risk during pregnancy

Anti-depressants

As we discussed earlier in chapter one, anti-depressants are not the most effective drugs for those with bipolar disorder. There are a number of different types of anti-depressants, but the two most commonly prescribed are the Trcyclic anti-depressants (TCA's) and the serotonin reuptake inhibitors (SSRI's). The first type has been in use a long time now and the second type for about ten years. Both are effective and both take between two weeks and a month to relieve depression. However, both types of drugs have differing side effects.

In bi-polar disorder, these drugs may be used during depressive episodes. However, as mentioned the side effects can present a danger. There is a risk, in some people that anti-depressants can trigger an episode of mania. People with bi-polar should probably be on a mood stabilizer if taking anti-depressants and, as a rule, not take them for more than six months.

The TCA's

Examples of these drugs include Amitriptyline (Lentizol/Elavil), dothiepin/dosulepin (prothiaden) and lofepramine (Gamanil).

Side effects of these drugs: they have a wide variety of side effects, which are often more pronounced during the early stages of taking the drug. Common side effects include tiredness and excessive sedation, dry mouth, constipation and difficulty in urinating. After the first few weeks, these side effects should decrease.

The SSRI's

Examples include fluoexetine (Prozac), paroxetine (Seroxat, paxil) citalopram (Cipramil, Cipram) and sertraline (Lustral, Zoloft). There are also some newer, related antidepressants, including venlafaxine (Efexor) and nefazodone (Dutonin). All of these drugs have weird and wonderful names, but some are more well know than others, such as Prozac, which has had a lot of bad press.

Side effects: these drugs are said to have fewer side effects than the trycyclics and are, supposedly, safer in the event of an overdose. However, they can have a number of varied side effects, including upset stomach, headaches, agitation and rashes. Like most side effects they subside over time.

One other class of anti-depressant that is sometimes prescribed is the monoamine oxidase (MAO) inhibitors. These were the first antidepressants, but most of them cannot be mixed with certain foods, such as cheeses and yeast products. For this reason, they are rarely prescribed. However, a new type of MAO inhibitor, moclobemide (Manerix) does not require dietary restriction.

Antipsychotic drugs (Neuroleptics)

Some anti-psychotic drugs are licensed for the treatment of mania. Their main use is in the treatment of psychosis and they have been shown to reduce or eliminate many of the symptoms of psychosis, such as delusions and hallucinations. In bi-polar disorder, they are used during acute manic episodes to calm the patient, slow racing thoughts and help with sleep. Some of the newer anti-psychotics have mood stabilizing properties. There are a number of different neuroleptics, such as: chlorpromazine (Largactil, Thorazine) haloperidol (Haldol) and trifluoperazine (Stelazine). Newer neuroleptics include risperidone (Risperdal) amisulpride (Solian) and olanzapine (Zyprexa) which are said to have fewer side effects and be easier to take.

Side-effects

All of the above drugs are associated with potentially serious side effects and should be used at the lowest effective dose for the shortest time. Side effects include sedation (sleepiness), dry mouth, weight gain, constipation and sensitivity to sunlight. A common class of side effects, the so-called extrapyramidal or parkinsonian side effects, include stiffness and restlessness.

Anti-parkinsonian drugs

These drugs are sometimes given with neuroleptics to relieve side effects. They are not prescribed initially, but only as a treatment for extrapyramidal side-effects if they develop. Anti-parkinsonian drugs include procyclidine (Kemadrin) benzatropine, (Cogentin) and benzhexol/trihexphenidl (Broflex). Side effects of these drugs can include dry mouth, stomach upsets, blurred vision and dizziness.

Minor tranquillisers

These medications, also known as *benzodiazepines* have been used for years to cure anxiety and insomnia. Valium is one of the better known but there are a number of other drugs within the same type. They provide quick relief from anxiety and sleeplessness and, if taken correctly, have fewer side effects. The main problem with these drugs is the risk of dependency. Common benzodiazepines include diazepam (Valium) lorazapam (Ativan) and clonazepam (Rivotril).

Medications and pregnancy

A number of medications for bipolar disorder can be associated with birth defects.

- Use effective birth control (contraception) to prevent pregnancy. Discuss birth control options with your doctor, as birth control medications may lose effectiveness when taken along with certain bipolar disorder medications.
- If you plan to become pregnant, meet with your doctor to discuss your treatment options.

- Discuss breast-feeding with your doctor, as some bipolar medications can pass through breast milk to your infant.

In the next chapter, we will look at professional help and support for those with bi-polar disorder.

Now read the main points from Chapter Three overleaf.

****

Main points from Chapter Three

❖ The National Institute for Health and Care Excellence (NICE) has guidelines for the treatment of bipolar disorder. They suggest that you should be offered structured psychological treatment while you are relatively stable but may be experiencing mild to moderate symptoms.

❖ Virtually everyone who has been diagnosed with bipolar disorder will receive medication of one sort or another. Although drugs cannot cure bi-polar disorder they help to manage the symptoms. When starting medication for bi-polar disorder, you should make sure that you know how to take it safely.

❖ During acute mania or depression you should talk with your doctor at least once a week, or more frequently, to monitor symptoms. As time goes by and you stabilise then you will see your GP less frequently.

4

Professional Help and Support

In this chapter, we will look at the professional help available for those with bipolar disorder. The range and types of help are many and varied. It is important that you choose the right one for you. In the first instance, bipolar disorder needs to be diagnosed by a psychiatrist, a professional who is medically trained to assess whether someone is suffering from a mental illness. The route to a psychiatrist is through your GP (see below).

Young people and bi-polar

If you are concerned that a young person under 18 may be developing bipolar, it is important to visit your GP and ask for an urgent referral to a specialist. A visit to the Child and Adolescent Mental Health Service (CAMHS) will be necessary, so the young person can be assessed and supported.

If the young person is over 18, they will need to ask for help themselves, from their GP.

Early intervention teams can help teenagers and young adults who are at risk of developing psychosis, which can be a feature of bipolar disorder – ask your GP about this service as it is not available in all areas.

If the child or young person is in a very distressed, violent or psychotic state or is at risk of harming themselves or others, you can take them to A&E and ask for an emergency psychiatric assessment. Alternatively you may need to ring the emergency services and ask them to visit the young person at home. They may have to be admitted to hospital under the Mental Health Act, for assessment and treatment.

YoungMinds Parents' Helpline is there for you if you want to talk about bipolar disorder and how to get your child the best help, Tel 0808 802 5544.

General practitioners-the first stop

You're likely to start by seeing your family doctor or a general practitioner. However, in some cases when you call to set up an appointment, you may be referred immediately to a medical doctor who specializes in diagnosing and treating mental health conditions (psychiatrist).

Because appointments can be brief, and because there's often a lot of ground to cover, it's a good idea to be well prepared for your appointment. Here's some information to help you get ready for your appointment, and know what to expect from your doctor.

What you can do

Write down any symptoms you've had, including any that may seem unrelated to the reason for which you scheduled the appointment.

- Write down key personal information, including any major stresses or recent life changes.
- Make a list of all medications, vitamins or supplements that you're taking.
- Take a family member or friend along, if possible. Sometimes it can be difficult to remember all of the information provided to you during an appointment. Someone who accompanies you may remember something that you missed or forgot.
- Write down questions to ask your doctor. Your time with your doctor may be limited, so preparing a list of questions ahead of time will help you make the most of your time together. For problems related to bipolar disorder, some basic questions to ask your doctor include:
- Do I have bipolar disorder?
- Are there any other possible causes for my symptoms?
- What kinds of tests will I need?
- What treatments are available? Which do you recommend for me?
- What side effects are possible with that treatment?
- What are the alternatives to the primary approach that you're suggesting?
- I have these other health conditions. How can I best manage these conditions together?
- Should I see a psychiatrist or other mental health provider?
- Is there a generic alternative to the medicine you're prescribing me?
- Are there any brochures or other printed material that I can take home with me? What websites do you recommend visiting?
- In addition to the questions that you've prepared to ask your doctor, don't hesitate to ask questions during your appointment at any time that you don't understand something.

What to expect from your doctor

In addition to your questions, your doctor is likely to ask you a number of questions. Being ready to answer them may reserve time to go over any points you want to spend more time on. Your doctor may ask:

- When did you or your loved ones first begin noticing your symptoms of depression, mania or hypomania?
- How frequently do your moods change?
- Do you ever have suicidal thoughts when you're feeling down?
- How severe are your symptoms? Do they interfere with your daily life or relationships?
- Do you have any blood relatives with bi-polar disorder or another mood disorder?
- What other mental or physical health conditions do you have?
- Do you drink alcohol, smoke cigarettes or use street drugs?
- How much do you sleep at night? Does it change over time?
- Do you go through periods when you take risks you wouldn't normally take, such as unsafe sex or unwise, spontaneous financial decisions?
- What, if anything, seems to improve your symptoms?
- What, if anything, appears to worsen your symptoms?
- Some alternative treatments may help, but there isn't much research on them. Most of the studies that do exist are on major depression, so it isn't clear how well most of these work for bipolar disorder.

Community mental health teams

If you have been referred to psychiatric services in England or Wales, by your GP, you have a right to get your needs assessed and a care plan developed for you within the Care Programme Approach (CPA). Your care plan should include a thorough assessment of your social and health care needs. You should be allocated a care-coordinator who is in charge of your care and ongoing reviews. You are entitled to say what your needs are and also to have an advocate present. An advocate is someone who can speak for you if necessary. More about CPA below.

Often, community care assessments are made by Community Mental Health Teams. Their aim is to help you live independently. They can also help with practical issues, such as sorting out welfare benefits if appropriate and also other services, such as day-centres, or drop in centres. They can also arrange for a Community Psychiatric Nurse (CPN) to visit your home.

Psychotherapy

Psychotherapy is another vital part of bipolar disorder treatment. Several types of therapy may be helpful. These include:

- **Cognitive behavioral therapy.** This is a common form of individual therapy for bipolar disorder. The focus of cognitive behavioral therapy is identifying unhealthy, negative beliefs and behaviors and replacing them with healthy, positive ones. It can help identify what triggers your bipolar episodes. You also learn effective strategies to manage stress and to cope with upsetting situations.
- **Psychoeducation.** Counselling to help you learn about bipolar disorder (psychoeducation) can help you and your loved ones understand bipolar disorder. Knowing what's going on can help you get the best support and treatment, and help you and your loved ones recognize warning signs of mood swings.

- **Family therapy.** Family therapy involves seeing a psychologist or other mental health provider along with your family members. Family therapy can help identify and reduce stress within your family. It can help your family learn how to communicate better, solve problems and resolve conflicts.
- **Group therapy.** Group therapy provides a forum to communicate with and learn from others in a similar situation. It may also help build better relationship skills.
- **Other therapies.** Other therapies that have been studied with some evidence of success include early identification and therapy for worsening symptoms (prodrome detection) and therapy to identify and resolve problems with your daily routine and interpersonal relationships (interpersonal and social rhythm therapy). Ask your doctor if any of these options may be appropriate for you.

Psychodynamic therapists

Psychodynamic theraprists have traditionally viewed psychological and psychiatric problems as originating in a person's childhood and development. Courses of therapy are usually longer than with cognitive behavioural therapy, and the therapy may focus less on specific problems and more on personal relationships. Psychodynamic therapists can be dotcors, psychologists or members of other professions. In addition to being funded by the NHS, it is possible to seek therapy privately.

Care co-ordinators

Over the last few decades, as medications have become more effective, it has become very unusual indeed for people with serious mental illness to spend very long periods in hospital.

More and more effeort has gone into helping people to live in the in the community. This approach has had varying degrees of success.

In the UK, one key part of this approach, called the care programme approach, calls for certain people to be monitored out in the community by a care co-ordinator who is usually either a nurse or a social worker. The care co-ordinator is supposed to meet with the patient regularly, offer advice and support and make sure that he or she is staying well and receiving guidance on taking medication and receiving all other services to which they may be entitled.

If a person is in receipt of benefits, or having financial problems, the care co-ordinator can offer practical support. The care co-ordinator is also supposed to convene regular meetings of all involved with the patients care, but this will only happen if the illness is very severe.

Hospitalization

In some cases, usually for short periods, people with bipolar disorder benefit from hospitalization. Getting psychiatric treatment at a hospital can help keep you calm and safe and stabilize your mood, whether you're having a manic episode or a deep depression. Partial hospitalization or day treatment programs also are options to consider. These programs provide the support and counselling you need while you get symptoms under control.

Now read the main points from chapter 4 overleaf

Main points from chapter 4

❖ In the first instance, bipolar disorder needs to be diagnosed by a psychiatrist, a professional who is medically trained to assess whether someone is suffering from a mental illness. The route to a psychiatrist is through your GP.

❖ If you are concerned that a young person under 18 may be developing bipolar, it is important to visit your GP and ask for an urgent referral to a specialist. A visit to the Child and Adolescent Mental Health Service (CAMHS) will be necessary, so the young person can be assessed and supported.

❖ In some cases when you call to set up an appointment, you may be referred immediately to a medical doctor who specializes in diagnosing and treating mental health conditions (psychiatrist). Because appointments can be brief, and because there's often a lot of ground to cover, it's a good idea to be well prepared for your appointment.

❖ Often, community care assessments are made by Community Mental Health Teams. Their aim is to help you live independently. They can also help with practical issues, such as sorting out welfare benefits if appropriate and also other services, such as day-centres, or drop in centres. They can also arrange for a community psychiatric nurse (CPN) to visit your home.

❖ Psychotherapy is another vital part of bipolar disorder treatment. Several types of therapy may be helpful such as cognitive behavioural therapy and family therapy. There are a range of other therapies.

5

More about Behavioural Therapies

We discussed the various therapies available to treat bipolar disorder in the last chapter. In this chapter we will expand on cognitive behavioural therapy as it is so important in the treatment of bipolar disorder..

As time has gone on, there has been a recognition that mood stabilisers (medications) fail a significant percentage of bi-polar patients. Therefore, there is room for improving the treatment of bi-polar disorder.

Almost all recent developments combine psychotherapy with medication in order to prevent relapses. These approaches are based on assumptions that although medications help the biological aspects of illness, psychotherapy is also needed to help the individual to lead a life that avoids unnecessary stress.

Two types of psychotherapy are being developed for bipolar patients: interpersonal therapy and cognitive behavioural therapy. It is on the latter that we will dwell as interpersonal therapy is still very much in the process of development.

What is cognitive behavioural therapy?

Cognitive therapy

Cognitive behavioural therapy (CBT) aims to help you to change the way that you think, feel and behave. It is used as a treatment for various mental health and physical problems. Our cognitive processes are our thoughts which include our ideas, mental images, beliefs and attitudes. Cognitive therapy is based on the principle that certain ways of thinking can trigger, or fuel, certain health problems. For example, anxiety, depression, phobias, etc, but there are others, including physical problems. The therapist helps you to understand your current thought patterns. In particular, to identify any harmful, unhelpful, and false ideas or thoughts which you have that can trigger your health problem, or make it worse. The aim is then to change your ways of thinking to avoid these ideas. Also, to help your thought patterns to be more realistic and helpful.

Behavioural therapy

This aims to change any behaviours that are harmful or not helpful. Various techniques are used. For example, a common unhelpful behaviour is to avoid situations that can make you anxious. In some people with phobias the avoidance can become extreme and affect day-to-day life. In this situation a type of behavioural therapy called exposure therapy may be used. This is where you are gradually exposed more and more to feared situations. The therapist teaches you how to control anxiety and to cope when you face up to the feared situations, for example, by using deep-breathing and other techniques.

Cognitive behavioural therapy (CBT)

This is a mixture of cognitive and behavioural therapies. They are often combined because how we behave often reflects how we think about certain things or situations.

The emphasis on cognitive or behavioural aspects of therapy can vary, depending on the condition being treated. For example, there is often more emphasis on behavioural therapy when treating obsessive-compulsive disorder (OCD) - where repetitive compulsive actions are a main problem. In contrast, the emphasis may be on cognitive therapy when treating depression.

What conditions can be helped by cognitive behavioural therapy?

CBT has been shown to help people with various conditions - both mental health conditions and physical conditions. As a rule, the more specific the problem, the more likely CBT may help. This is because it is a practical therapy which focuses on particular problems and aims to overcome them. CBT is sometimes used alone, and sometimes used in addition to medication, depending on the type and severity of the condition being treated.

What is likely to happen during a course of cognitive behavioural therapy?

The first session of therapy will usually include time for the therapist and you to develop a shared understanding of the problem. This is usually to identify how your thoughts, ideas, feelings, attitudes, and behaviours affect your day-to-day life.

You should then agree a treatment plan and goals to achieve, and the number of sessions likely to be needed. Each session lasts about 50-60 minutes. Typically, a session of therapy is done once a week. Most courses of CBT last for several weeks. It is common to have 10-15 sessions, but a course of CBT can be longer or shorter, depending on the nature and severity of the condition. In some situations CBT sessions can be done by telephone.

You have to take an active part, and are given homework between sessions. For example, if you have social phobia, early in the course of therapy you may be asked to keep a diary of your thoughts which occur when you become anxious before a social event. Later on you may be given homework of trying out ways of coping which you have learned during therapy.

How well does cognitive behavioural therapy work?

CBT has been shown in clinical trials to help ease symptoms of various health problems. For example, research studies have shown that a course of CBT is just as likely to be effective as medication in treating depression and certain anxiety disorders. There may be long-term benefits of CBT, as the techniques to combat these problems can be used for the rest of your life to help to keep symptoms away. So, for example, depression or anxiety are less likely to recur in the future.

CBT is one type of psychotherapy (talking treatment). Unlike other types of psychotherapy it does not involve talking freely, or dwell on events in your past to gain insight into your emotional state of mind. It is not a "lie on the couch and tell all" type of therapy.

CBT tends to deal with the here and now - how your current thoughts and behaviours are affecting you now. It recognises that events in your past have shaped the way that you currently think and behave. In particular, thought patterns and behaviours learned in childhood, However, CBT does not dwell on the past, but aims to find solutions to how to change your current thoughts and behaviours so that you can function better now and in the future.

CBT is also different to counselling, which is meant to be non-directive, empathetic and supportive. Although the CBT therapist will offer support and empathy, the therapy has a structure, is problem-focused and practical.

What are the limitations of cognitive behavioural therapy?

CBT does not suit everyone and it is not helpful for all conditions. You need to be committed and persistent in tackling and improving your health problem with the help of the therapist. It can be hard work. The homework may be difficult and challenging. You may be taken 'out of your comfort zone' when tackling situations which cause anxiety or distress. However, many people have greatly benefited from a course of CBT.

How can I get cognitive behavioural therapy?

Your doctor may refer you to a therapist who has been trained in CBT. This may be a psychologist, psychiatrist, psychiatric nurse, or other healthcare professional. There is a limited number of CBT therapists available on the NHS. You may wish to go privately if it is not available in your area on the NHS. However, government policy is to make CBT more widely available on the NHS.

Do-it-yourself cognitive behavioural therapy

Although CBT with the help of a trained therapist is best, some people prefer to tackle their problems themselves. There are a range of books and leaflets on self-help for the problems which CBT is useful for (anxiety, phobias, depression, etc). More recently, interactive CDs and websites are being developed and evaluated for self-directed CBT for a variety of conditions.

In the next chapter, we will be taking a look of the effects of stigma and shame on bipolar sufferers and how to deal with this.

Now read the main points from Chapter 5 overleaf

****

Main points from chapter 5

❖ As time has gone on, there has been a recognition that mood stabilisers (medications) fail a significant percentage of bipolar patients. Therefore, there is room for improving the treatment of bipolar disorder.

❖ Almost all recent developments combine psychotherapy with medication in order to prevent relapses. These approaches are based on assumptions that although medications help the biological aspects of illness, psychotherapy is also needed to help the individual to lead a life that avoids unnecessary stress.

❖ Cognitive Behavioural Therapy (CBT) aims to help you to change the way that you think, feel and behave. It is used as a treatment for various mental health and physical problems

❖ Your doctor may refer you to a therapist who has been trained in CBT. This may be a psychologist, psychiatrist, psychiatric nurse, or other healthcare professional. There is a limited number of CBT therapists available on the NHS. You may wish to go privately if it is not available in your area on the NHS.

6

Dealing With Stigma and Shame

Bipolar- Stigmatisation and Feelings of Shame

Illnesses generally cause distress and discomfort, including physical pain and mental discomfort. However, some illnesses, such as bipolar disorder can cause additional problems by affecting the way we feel about ourselves around other people. Sufferers may feel ashamed or embarrassed to admit their diagnoses because of the reactions of others.

Everyone should have the right to decide when and with whom to disclose health problems. In some cases, privacy can be both appropriate and desirable. There is a difference, however, between illnesses we choose to keep private simply out of personal preference and those that we feel we must keep private in order to preserve our social standing, our jobs or our legal rights. When we feel that we have to keep our illness a secret, as do many with psychological disorders, we are feeling the effects of stigma.

Stigma

Stigma is a term used to describe two things, a feeling of prejudice or dislike towards some group on the part of the general population, and the corresponding feeling of shame caused in that group by that prejudice. The stigmatisation of the mentally ill is rife and has been much studied. This stigmatisation is caused by ignorance and fear of outsiders, those who do not suffer from bipolar disorder.

Effects of stigma

Stigma seems to affect sufferers in two ways: through their reaction to others and through their feelings about themselves. Some sufferers worry about the reaction of others, fearing that they might not be accepted, or that other people will think of them as 'mad'. Alternatively, some people are more affected by internal feelings of shame and worthlessness, the feeling that they are deeply flawed.

Inner feelings of stigmatisation can produce a sense of low self-worth: you may feel damaged or inferior in some way. Such a feeling can be combated in various ways and careful thought about one's own personal state is necessary.

Plenty of illnesses, including HIV and hepatitis, can be stigmatising. When it comes to mental disorders, however, stigma and shame can operate in a couple of unique ways.

- Those with common psychological disorders, especially depression and anxiety, frequently feel bad about themselves to begin with. That's one of the primary identifying symptoms of these illnesses. Therefore, stigma about mental illness feeds into their psychological symptoms, which can in turn worsen feelings of stigma and shame.
- Depression, anxiety and bipolar disorder can cause people to behave in ways that they usually wouldn't. They might miss or break important appointments. badly. They

might drink more, take drugs, spend compulsively or engage in other obsessive behaviours. Often, they try to keep their worst behaviour a secret from those around them. All of this exacerbates underlying feelings of shame and guilt and can cause others to judge them harshly.

When all of this is taken together, it is completely understandable if we want to tell no one about our illness. Unfortunately, trying to cope with mental illness without the help and support of others can hinder our recovery and keep us from getting care we might need.

The first step away from the negative feedback loop of stigma and shame comes in the form of information, information about how common psychological problems are, how effective treatment can be, and how likely it is that those with mental disorders will lead rich and fulfilling lives.

Another important step is seeking qualified help. Effective treatment-psychological, medical and social-makes a huge difference in terms of our symptoms and how we feel about ourselves. Receiving a formal diagnosis of a mental disorder might bring up feelings of stigma and shame. Some people fear that this forever marks them as different from everyone else, or that they can never lead a normal and happy life. This doesn't have to be the case.

A diagnosis is a label that professionals use to help determine the proper course of treatment. The diagnosis, however, doesn't define you. It defines the problem and how you and your doctor can combat it.

Telling people you trust about your problem will also help fight stigma and shame. This can start with your primary health care provider or your mental health care provider. Ultimately, sharing what you've been through with close friends and family, or with other people who have struggled with the same illness, can be both a freeing and healing experience. Disclosure must be approached cautiously, but it can be an effective tool not only to break out of isolation, but also to restore feelings of self-confidence.

Freedom from stigma can also come from examining your life and values then figuring out how to overcome your limitations and give back to the world in a way that is meaningful to you. For some, this might mean spending more time with children or grandchildren, or helping friends and neighbours. For others, it might mean engaging in volunteer or church work. Still others find satisfaction and fulfilment in telling their story more publicly or in helping others who are struggling with mental illness. Ultimately, the more that people like us talk openly about our illness, the more that stigma will fade away-not just from our own lives, but also from society at large.

Finally, of course bi-polar disorder can be a disabling and distressing illness. In this it is similar to many other disabilities. few people would choose to be blind or without a limb but this does not mean that a disabled person is of less worth than others. A humane society, which hopefully we are in, is one with opportunity for all.

In the final analysis, the best way of combating the sense of stigma is to first obtain all the help that you can, and then to work to make your life as fulfilled as possible. There is much people with bipolar can do to diminish the bad effects of the illness and lead fulfilling lives.

In the next chapter, we will look at bipolar disorder and the nature and effect of vicious cycles.

Now read the main points from Chapter 6 overleaf

****

Main points from Chapter 6

❖ Illnesses generally cause distress and discomfort, including physical pain and mental discomfort. However, some illnesses, such as bipolar disorder can cause additional problems by affecting the way we feel about ourselves around other people. Stigmatisation and shame may arise as a result of these negative feelings.

❖ Inner feelings of stigmatisation can produce a sense of low self-worth: you may feel damaged or inferior in some way. Such a feeling can be combated in various ways and careful thought about one's own personal state is necessary.

❖ The first step away from the negative feedback loop of stigma and shame comes in the form of information, information about how common psychological problems are, how effective treatment can be, and how likely it is that those with mental disorders will lead rich and fulfilling lives.

❖ In the final analysis, the best way of combating the sense of stigma is to first obtain all the help that you can, and then to work to make your life as fulfilled as possible

7

Bipolar Disorder and Vicious Cycles

Bipolar Disorder and Vicious Cycles

Vicious cycles are often found to play an important role in a variety of everyday psychological problems, but especially in bipolar disorder. This is when one thing leads to another and then back again. For example, in alcoholics, one drink may lead to another and another, and afterward they feel ashamed or depressed, only to use that as an excuse to start drinking again. Then it's like a vicious cycle, repeating itself.

This can happen to people with bipolar disorder as well. For example, procrastination is a very common problem for people with the disorder. Procrastination can also set up a vicious cycle – the more you delay dealing with your problems and tasks, the more difficult they begin to seem, so you put off doing them further, which is more procrastination.

This happens during bipolar episodes, someone in a manic episode can feel powerful, attractive, successful, etc. Because they "feel" energetic, they decline the need for sleep. Then sleep deprivation makes the manic episode worse, and they are in a vicious cycle.

On the other hand, someone in a depressive episode can feel worthless, helpless, hopeless, likely to fail, etc. This leads to inactivity, more sleep, and isolation, which are all triggers for episodes, so the vicious cycle continues.

The first step to breaking out of a vicious cycle is to recognize that you are in one.

Vicious cycles and stress

As we have seen in the earlier chapters, stress is the enemy of the person with bipolar disorder. Life is stressful enough for everyone, particularly in this modern age where housing and employment is becoming more difficult to access and life in general is harder than it was.

Although a certain amount of stress can be positive, it is where the stress becomes excessive that leads to vicious cycles. You might be faced with multiple demands, feel anxious, nervous and tense and you might procrastinate and not meet these demands, which leads you into a vicious cycle as the situation can only get worse.

The first thing that you have to do is to make sure that you are organised and that everything is down in black and white and that you can follow your script-i.e. you have a list of things that you need to do and do them, to avoid problems piling up.

Relaxation

Stress can cause all sorts of problems, not least physical. problems can include excessive sweating, restlessness, stomach problems and rapid heartbeat. Stress can also lead to lack of sleep due to worry the best way to combat these particular side effects is by adopting certain relaxation techniques. A variety of tried and tested techniques can be used.

Breathing Exercise

This relaxation technique can be very a potent weapon against anxiety or panic attacks. it can also be used during a manic phase of Bipolar disorder. Doing this exercise before laying down to go to sleep may help with insomnia in some people.

When experiencing a panic attack it is best if possible, to close your mouth and breathe through your nose to avoid hyperventilation.

It is also advisable any time you practice breathing exercises to either sit or lie down to prevent passing out, or falling due to dizziness.

Many people find it useful to do these exercises before they begin visualization, or meditation to help them relax. Also, many people find positive self-talk useful in conjunction with these exercises. Such as calmly saying short phrases like " Let it go" or "It's all ok " silently to yourself while exhaling.

The idea is to get yourself to relax as much as possible. Trying to relax or judge your performance may be counter-productive, so clear your mind of everything except your positive self talk or counting between breaths.

Note the amount of tension you are feeling, and let it go as much as possible while exhaling slowly through your nose or mouth. (Again, if you are having a panic attack, it is best to keep your mouth closed.) Then breathe slowly and deeply into your abdomen. (You will know you are doing this correctly if you place your hand on your abdomen and feel it rising as you breathe in.)

Hold the breath for a count of 2-5 seconds (whatever you are more comfortable with.. the longer you hold the more you will relax when you exhale.. but to prevent passing out you should not hold it any longer than 5 seconds)

Exhale again, slowly for anywhere between 5 and 10 seconds.

Repeat breathing this way until your anxiety subsides, or you feel properly relaxed.

Progressive Muscle Relaxation

If you have anxiety disorder it is advisable to do this exercise every day. When you start out , it is best to do this for around 20 minutes. As you gain skill in relaxation technique the amount of time you need will diminish.

Find a quiet place to practice in. If you feel the need to play music, choose relaxing instrumental music. If you play music that has lyrics, it may distract you, or work to govern your mood.

Try to do this at the same time every day. If you suffer from insomnia, you may find it helpful to do this before bed.

Make sure you are neither hungry or overfull. Also make sure you are in a comfortable position, wearing comfortable clothing, and you take off your shoes, jewellery, glasses, contacts, etc.

Make a decision to not worry about anything during this time. Make peace of mind for this amount of time a priority every day.

As with the breathing exercise, it is not necessary to judge your performance or try to relax. This is your time every day to just "let go".

Once you are comfortable and relaxed, (you may want to do the breathing exercise first) start by curling and tensing your toes. Tense them hard enough to feel it, but not hard enough that you feel strained. Hold the tension for about ten seconds, concentrating on how it feels and then let it go. Stop for a moment to notice the difference between how they felt when they were tensed and how they feel relaxed.

Next, curl and tense your feet, concentrate on how they feel, hold the tension for about 10 seconds and release. Notice the difference. Next tense your calves, continue this process of tensing and releasing the muscles all the way up your body, thighs, buttocks, abdomen, back,(by gently arching it) fists, lower arms, upper arms, shoulders, neck,(by gently lifting your head, holding it up and then gently laying it back down)and face (scrunch it up ... nobody is looking).

Repeat this process beginning with your face, and progressing back down to your toes. Now would be a good time to also repeat the breathing exercise.

Visualization

After completing the breathing and progressive muscle relaxation exercises, you may want to do some visualization. This is a bit like meditation.

Design a peaceful scene for yourself. It may be helpful to write it out on a piece of paper and study it before you begin. Your scene can be anywhere you choose. At home in front of a cosy fire, or at the ocean. It's up to you. The only thing you need to worry about, is that there is enough detail involved in your scene to absorb your full attention.

Here is an example:

I am lying on a soft grassy spot along the bank of a rushing river in the woods. It is a warm summer evening at dusk. There is a purple ribbon of colour just above a mountain as the sun finishes setting behind it. I can hear the water rushing beside me , and feel a slight mist of water spraying over me in contrast to the warm breeze that is blowing the fragrance of water, pine and wild flowers over me as well. I can hear birds chirping in the tall pine trees, and the wood crackling in the camp fire that is burning not too far away. As I watch the smoke rising from the campfire into the navy blue sky, I begin to see stars appearing overhead.

You may wish to record your peaceful scene onto a tape so that you can visualize it without effort. After you become comfortable with returning to your scene, you can practice going there to do your progressive muscle relaxation or breathing exercises.

Again, doing this every day will be helpful with reducing stress and helping you relax. Doing these relaxation exercises before bedtime, may help reduce the symptoms of insomnia.

The vicious cycle of anger and controlling anger

Expressing anger is a normal human emotion that everyone experiences to varying degrees. Bipolar Disorder sufferers however, are especially prone to experiencing extreme mood swings, changeable behaviour patterns and irritable symptoms because this combination is a prominent aspect of the disorder. Accepting the emotional challenges that compromise behaviour, when living with Bipolar Disorder, may help achieve better understanding of the anger expressed.

Understanding Your Anger Pattern

If you live with Bipolar Disorder, then you will understand only too well that the mild or severe shift in mood impacts on everyday life and can create aggressive and excessive behaviour and also depressive symptoms. This negative pattern affects individuals in many ways and severe agitation and anger may also develop during manic periods.

It is very important indeed to clearly identify your anger pattern. By doing so you will be more able to avoid negative triggers and to create positive changes where appropriate. You will also be able to understand how stress and life events affect you, and how fear and resentment also play a part in maintaining a negative outlook. Once you are able to understand your anger pattern you will be able to learn ways of alternative responses. One of the most important responses is to stop and reflect, if possible, take a deep breath and draw back. Quite often, during episodes of mania, sudden anger will lead to actions that cause regret, can even lead to grave problems after the event.

Suppressing Anger

Viewing things and situations from a negative perspective is both destructive and restrictive. Bipolar disorder predisposes sufferers to manic behaviour symptoms that can create continually negative patterns of mood swing that impact on anger, stress and frustration. If these emotions are suppressed in a negative manner, through bottling up and turning feelings inwards, the outcome and consequences become more escalated and unmanageable. If, however, anger is channelled in a constructive and positive way the extreme emotions can become easier to manage.

Learning to express feelings in a calm manner is healthy and important in making improvements in the effective, positive suppression of anger. Using calming strategies with the aid of relaxation and breathing techniques as described above, will help to reduce inner turmoil and maintain neutral behaviour. Exercising regularly and using visualisation techniques, during relaxation periods, also works well in creating a positive change in behaviour.

To summarise, things you and/or your partner can do to minimise the impact of vicious cycles are:

1.   Avoid stress – this is the biggest trigger to a vicious cycle.

2.   Stay active.

3.   Be productive – but not excessively.

4.   Communicate with each other.

5.   Help each other recognize the other one's vicious cycles.

6.   Consciously face the vicious cycle.

7.   Replace negative thoughts with positive thoughts.

8.   Think all the way through things before you do them.

The more you and/or your spouse can make fighting vicious cycles a conscious thing, the better off you will be, instead of just reacting, or acting impulsively, which makes a vicious cycle worse.

In the next chapter, we will deal with one other important element in dealing with vicious cycles that is well worth mentioning, and that is an understanding of **assertiveness** and how this impacts on you as an individual.

Now read the main points from Chapter 7 overleaf.

****

Main points from chapter 7

❖ Vicious cycles are often found to play an important role in a variety of everyday psychological problems, but especially in bipolar disorder. This is when one thing leads to another and then back again. For example, in alcoholics, one drink may lead to another and another, and afterward they feel ashamed or depressed, only to use that as an excuse to start drinking again. Then it's like a vicious cycle, repeating itself.

❖ Procrastination is a very common problem for people with the disorder. Procrastination can also set up a vicious cycle – the more you delay dealing with your problems and tasks, the more difficult they begin to seem, so you put off doing them further, which is more procrastination.

❖ Stress can cause all sorts of problems, not least physical. problems can include excessive sweating, restlessness, stomach problems and rapid heartbeat. Stress can also lead to lack of sleep due to worry the best way to combat these particular side effects is by adopting certain relaxation techniques. A variety of tried and tested techniques can be used such as breathing exercises and progressive muscle relaxation.

❖ Anger is one emotion that gives rise to a vicious cycle and must be controlled. This can be achieved through the understanding of your anger patterns and learning to express feelings in a calm manner.

8

Assertiveness-The Importance of Being Assertive in the Control of Vicious Cycles

---

Understanding the concept of assertiveness and the need for bi-polar sufferers in particular to be assertive but not aggressive is essential to controlling situations and avoiding vicious cycles.

Assertiveness is not a personality trait which persists consistently across all situations. Different individuals exhibit varying degrees of assertive behaviour depending on whether they are in a work, social, academic, recreational or relationship context.

The most important point to remember is that there is a big difference between being assertive and standing up for yourself, and being aggressive.

Non-Assertiveness

A non-assertive person is one who is often taken advantage of, feels helpless, takes on everyone's problems, says yes to inappropriate demands and thoughtless requests, and allows others to choose for him or her. However, the non-assertive person can get angry if he or she feels ignored or in any way a victim of injustice.

The non-assertive person is emotionally dishonest, indirect, self-denying, and inhibited. He/she feels hurt, anxious, and possibly angry about his/her actions.

Non-Assertive Body Language:

- Lack of eye contact; looking down or away.
- Swaying and shifting of weight from one foot to the other.
- Whining and hesitancy when speaking.

Assertiveness

An assertive person is one who acts in his/her own best interests, stands up for self, expresses feelings honestly, is in charge of self in interpersonal relations, and chooses for self.

An assertive person is emotionally honest, direct, self-enhancing, and expressive. He/she feels confident, self-respecting at the time of his/her actions as well as later. There is a big difference between being assertive and being aggressive.

Assertive Body Language:

- Stand straight, steady, and directly face the people to whom you are speaking while maintaining eye contact.
- Speak in a clear, steady voice - loud enough for the people to whom you are speaking to hear you.
- Speak fluently, without hesitation, and with assurance and confidence.

Aggressiveness

An aggressive person is one who wins by using power, hurts others, is intimidating, controls the environment to suit his/her needs, and chooses for others.

He/she is inappropriately expressive, emotionally honest, direct, and self-enhancing at the expense of another. An aggressive person feels righteous, superior, deprecatory at the time of action and possibly guilty later.

Aggressive Body Language:

- Leaning forward with glaring eyes.
- Pointing a finger at the person to whom you are speaking.
- Shouting.
- Clenching the fists.
- Putting hands on hips and wagging the head.

How To Improve the Communication Process

- Active listening: reflecting back (paraphrasing) to the other person
- Identifying your position: stating your thoughts and feelings about the situation.

Assertive Ways of Saying "No":

- Basic principles to follow in answers: brevity, clarity, firmness, and honesty.
- Begin your answer with the word "NO" so it is not ambiguous.
- Make your answer short and to the point.

- Don't give a long explanation.
- Be honest, direct and firm.
- Don't say, "I'm sorry, but..."

The above is just an outline of assertiveness techniques. It is very wise to give a lot of thought to your approach to anger management and also assertiveness techniques. There are lots of organisations offering advice in this area and several are listed in the useful addresses and websites section at the end of this book.

In the next chapter, we will explore the risks of sleep loss and its effects on bipolar disorder.

Now read the main points from Chapter 8 overleaf

****

Main points from Chapter 8

❖ Understanding the concept of assertiveness and the need for bi-polar sufferers in particular to be assertive but not aggressive is essential to controlling situations and avoiding vicious cycles.

❖ The most important point to remember is that there is a big difference between being assertive and standing up for yourself, and being aggressive.

❖ A non-assertive person is one who is often taken advantage of, feels helpless, takes on everyone's problems, says yes to inappropriate demands and thoughtless requests, and allows others to choose for him or her.

❖ An assertive person is one who acts in his/her own best interests, stands up for self, expresses feelings honestly, is in charge of self in interpersonal relations, and chooses for self.

❖ An aggressive person is one who wins by using power, hurts others, is intimidating, controls the environment to suit his/her needs, and chooses for others.

❖ Being assertive will help enormously in the process of combating vicious cycles and also achieving self-confidence.

9

The Risks of Sleep Loss

We have established at the beginning of this book how important sleep is to the maintenance of the health of bipolar sufferers. Many people have problems with sleep, some more than others. However, for those with bipolar disorder sleep is of the utmost importance. This can be a vicious circle as the very fact that a person suffers from bipolar often means that sleep patterns will be disturbed.

How bipolar disorder affects sleep

Bipolar disorder may affect sleep in many ways. For example it can lead to:

- Insomnia is the inability to fall asleep or remain asleep long enough to feel rested.
- Delayed sleep phase syndrome, a circadian-rhythm sleep disorder resulting in insomnia and daytime sleepiness.
- REM (rapid eye movement) sleep abnormalities, which may make dreams very vivid or bizarre.
- Irregular sleep-wake schedules, which sometimes results from a lifestyle that involves medication-seeking behaviour at night.

During the lows of bipolar disorder, you may have overwhelming feelings of hopelessness, sadness and worthlessness. These can interfere with your sleep. During the highs of bipolar disorder (periods of mania), you may be so aroused that you can go for days without sleep. For three in four people with bipolar disorder, sleep problems are the most common signal that a period of mania is about to occur.

When sleep is in short supply, someone with bipolar disorder may not miss it the way other people would. However, even though you seem to get by on so little sleep, lack of sleep can take quite a toll.

For example you may:

- Be extremely moody
- Feel sick, tired, depressed or worried
- Have trouble concentrating or making decisions
- Be at higher risk of an accidental death

Get better sleep with bipolar disorder

Disrupted sleep can really aggravate a mood disorder. A first step might involve figuring out all the factors that may be affecting sleep and discussing them with the doctor. Keeping a sleep diary may help. Include information about:

- How long it takes to go to sleep
- How many times you wake up during the night
- How long you sleep all night
- When you take medication or use caffeine, alcohol or nicotine
- When you exercise and for how long

Certain bipolar medications may also affect sleep as a side effect. For example, they may disrupt the sleep-wake cycle. One way to address this is to move bedtime and waking time later and later each day until you reach your desired goal. Another way to handle this situation is with bright light therapy.

Of course your doctor may recommend a change in medication if needed. Be sure to discuss any other medicines or medical conditions that may be affecting your sleep, such as arthritis, migraines or a back injury.

Restoring a regular schedule of daily activities and sleep - perhaps with the help of cognitive behavioural therapy - can go a long way towards helping restore more even moods.

Ways to get better sleep

A lot of people have trouble sleeping from time to time. However, you can make it easier to get a good night's sleep every night with these simple steps:

Cut caffeine. Caffeine can keep you awake. It can stay in your body longer than you might think - the effects of caffeine can take as long as eight hours to wear off. So if you drink a cup of coffee in the afternoon and are still tossing at night, caffeine might be the reason. Cutting out caffeine at least four to six hours before bedtime can help you fall asleep more easily.

Avoid alcohol as a sleep aid. Alcohol may initially help you fall asleep, but it also causes disturbances in sleep resulting in less restful sleep. An alcoholic drink before bedtime may make it more likely that you will wake up during the night.

Relax before bedtime. Stress not only makes you miserable, it wreaks havoc on your sleep. Develop some kind of pre-sleep ritual to break the connection between all the day's stress and bedtime. These rituals can be as short as 10 minutes or as long as an hour. Some people find relief in making a list of all the stressful things that have happened during the day, along with a plan to deal with them. This can act as "closure" to the day. Combining this with a period of relaxation perhaps by reading something light, meditating, aromatherapy, light stretching or taking a hot bath can also help you get better sleep. Also, don't look at the clock!

Exercise at the right time for you. Regular exercise can help you get a good night's sleep. The timing and intensity of exercise seems to play a key role in its effects on sleep. If you are the type of person who gets energised or becomes more alert after exercise, it may be best not to exercise in the evening. Regular exercise in the morning even can help relieve insomnia, according to a study.

Keep your bedroom quiet, dark and comfortable. For many people, even the slightest noise or light can disturb sleep like the purring of a cat or the light from your laptop or TV. Consider using earplugs, window blinds or curtains and an electric blanket - everything possible to create an ideal sleep environment. Don't use the overhead light if you need to get up at night; use a small night-light instead. Ideal room temperatures for sleeping are between 15C and 22C (59F and 71F). Temperatures above 24C (75F) or below about 12C (53F) can disrupt sleep.

Eat right, sleep tight. Try not to go to bed hungry, but avoid heavy meals before bedtime. An over-full stomach can keep you up, but some people believe certain foods can help. Milk contains tryptophan, which limited research suggests may, but is not proven to be, a sleep-promoting chemical or natural sedative. Foods like poultry, bananas, oats and honey contain tryptophan. Carbohydrate-rich foods like bread and crackers may complement dairy foods like milk, by increasing the level of tryptophan in the blood. Meanwhile, try not to drink fluids after 8pm. This can keep you from having to get up to use the toilet

Restrict nicotine. Having a smoke before bed - although it feels relaxing actually puts a stimulant into your bloodstream. The effects of nicotine are similar to those of caffeine. Nicotine can keep you up and awaken you at night. It should be avoided particularly near bedtime and if you wake up in the middle of the night.

Avoid napping. Napping may make matters worse if you usually have problems falling asleep. If you do nap, keep it short. A brief 15 to 20 minute snooze about eight hours after you get up in the morning can actually be rejuvenating.

Keep pets off the bed. If a pet sleeps with you then this, too, may cause you to awaken during the night, either from allergies or pet movements. Fido and Fluffy might be better off on the floor than on your sheets.

Avoid watching TV, eating and discussing emotional issues in bed. The bed should be used for sleep (and sex) only. If not, you can end up associating the bed with distracting activities that could make it difficult for you to fall asleep.

In the next chapter we will look at bipolar and issues within the family.

Now read the main points from Chapter 9 overleaf

****

Main points from Chapter 9

❖ Bipolar disorder may affect sleep in many ways. For example it can lead to insomnia, delayed sleep phase syndrome, REM (rapid eye movement) and irregular sleep-wake schedules.

❖ Disrupted sleep can really aggravate a mood disorder. A first step might involve figuring out all the factors that may be affecting sleep and discussing them with the doctor. Keeping a sleep diary may help.

❖ A lot of people have trouble sleeping from time to time. However, you can make it easier to get a good night's sleep every night with simple steps as described in chapter 9.

10

Bipolar Disorder-Family Issues

If you have been diagnosed with bipolar disorder, your family will be involved right from the outset. Having bipolar disorder will not prevent you from leaving home, and it is a fact that most sufferers manage to leave home and live independent lives. Some people have managed to maintain stable relationships. However, whatever the circumstance, it is almost certain that family will stay involved. Sometimes, this involvement arises out of feelings of guilt because family feel that they may have passed the problem on genetically.

Although parental support can be very welcome in the first instance, particularly helping a person access appropriate care at the beginning of the illness, it can be difficult determining levels of involvement as time moves on. Over-involvement can cause resentment in the sufferer, particularly if the sufferer perceives this involvement as interference in their life. It can be a difficult balance to strike.

With younger adults, parents will no doubt be concerned with a persons social competence in managing money and dealing with friends and also issues such as employment and dealing with others generally. Parents can also be concerned about sexuality, as a young person with bipolar may be vulnerable which can lead to unprotected sex, and the attendant problems with this, such as AIDS and other diseases.

Over-vigilance can be counter productive and it is probably best for parents and the person suffering from bipolar to discuss openly the problems and the best ways to tackle them. If this cannot, for some reason, be achieved then there are professional counsellors who will assist with the process. See the useful addresses at the back of the book.

Involvement of spouses and partners

Spouses and partners of bipolar sufferers are directly involved on a day-to-day basis. However, they also have their own feelings to cope with at the same time. Some spouses or partners may have formed a relationship with a bipolar sufferer in the full knowledge that they have that condition and accepted this as a 'part of the package'. However, from experience, in many cases it has to be said that bipolar disorder becomes apparent after people get together and this causes complications.

Grief and anger can arise, for both partners, as the problem unfolds and it becomes obvious that the future that you had envisaged together will not go according to plan. There can also be feelings of anger and resentment if one person feels that they weren't informed by the other that a condition existed. It is very important, even crucial, for both partners to respect the views of each other and to try to work through problems and arrive at a form of communication between each other. This will help provide a resolution to the problems that have arisen or are unfolding.

There are many support groups out there which will prove crucial in the maintenance of relationships between couples. These groups often consist of people who have been though the experience and can pass on first hand knowledge.

Family members, whether spouse, partner or parent can have a vital role in helping sufferers notice early signs of episodes so that they can use psychological skills to avert further problems or seek help from their mental health team. However, a balance needs to be drawn between this positive role and the risk of friction between family members if they are seen to be over-sensitive to even small changes in the behaviour of the person with bi-polar disorder. This balance involves a recognition that all people experience fluctuating mood states, including anger, happiness, frustration boredom and excitement. Thus, evidence of irritability in someone with bi-polar disorder is not necessarily a sign of anything other than their being irritated by an event in a normal way.

Family breakdown after illness and rebuilding relationships

In bipolar disorder there are two types of problem that can affect sufferers and their families. Having to cope with the problems of both depression and mania can be harder to understand for carers and spouses than dealing with depression in isolation. These episodes can cause significant problems for the family. Some symptoms of both depression and mania can be perceived as malicious and intentional. This is where real problems can start and can cause rifts and break up of relationships.

Sufferers are always advised to attempt to rebuild relationships that have suffered as a result of these episodes, when they are well. Also, clinical professionals may be crucial here in helping families understand and to be educated about the nature of the episodes and realise that they are not really malicious but are a result of the condition.

It is advised that, when the sufferer is well they should put in as much time as possible in rebuilding trust and repairing damaged relationships and also mending ill-feelings.

At times, a family can be particularly resentful if they perceive an episode as having been triggered by a sufferer's stopping his or her mood stabilisers. In this case, families see their sick relative as being irresponsible.. Family education is important here which involves professionals. They will make it clear that sometimes it is hard to judge whether sufferers stopped taking medication and then relapsed or whether they were in an early state of relapse when they stopped taking medication.

Families will almost certainly feel resentful if they see their relative or spouse abusing themselves with alcohol or drugs which fly's in the face of good advice. It is up to family to put their foot down if this happens and point out that this type of counter-productive behaviour is jeopardising their relationship with each other.

In the next chapter, we will be looking at the impact of diet on bipolar.

Now read the main points from Chapter 10 overleaf

****

Main points from Chapter 10

❖ If you have been diagnosed with bipolar disorder, your family will be involved right from the outset

❖ Although parental support can be very welcome in the first instance, particularly helping a person access appropriate care at the beginning of the illness, it can be difficult determining levels of involvement as time moves on.

❖ Spouses and partners of bipolar sufferers are directly involved on a day-to-day basis. However, they also have their own feelings to cope with at the same time

❖ Grief and anger can arise, for both partners, as the problem unfolds and it becomes obvious that the future that you had envisaged together will not go according to plan.

❖ It is very important, even crucial, for both partners to respect the views of each other and to try to work through problems and arrive at a form of communication between each other. This will help provide a resolution to the problems that have arisen or are unfolding.

❖ There are many support groups out there which will prove crucial in the maintenance of relationships between couples and other family members.

11

Bipolar Disorder and Diet

Is there a specific diet for people with Bipolar Disorder?

The first thing to emphasise is that there is no specific bipolar diet. Nevertheless, it is very important indeed to make wise dietary choices that will help you maintain a healthy weight and stay well. This applies to all people, whether bipolar sufferers or not.

These choices include:

- Avoiding the "Western" style diet that is rich in red meats, saturated fats and trans-fat and simple carbohydrates. This eating style is linked to a higher risk for obesity, type 2 diabetes, and heart disease. Eating less saturated fats and simple carbohydrates can help overall health but does not directly affect the symptoms of bipolar disorder.
- Eating a balance of protective, nutrient-dense foods. These foods include fresh fruits, vegetables, legumes, whole grains, lean meats, cold-water fish, eggs, low-fat dairy, soy products, and nuts and seeds. These foods provide the levels of nutrients necessary to maintain good health and prevent disease.
- Watching caloric intake and exercising regularly to maintain a healthy weight. Some findings show that those with bipolar disorder may have a greater risk of being

overweight or obese. Talk to your doctor about ways to avoid weight gain when taking bipolar medications.

Does Fish Oil Improve Mood With Bipolar Disorder?

It is generally acknowledged that eating fatty fish at least two times a week is good for most people. Good choices include:

- Albacore tuna
- Herring
- Mackerel
- Salmon
- Trout

If you do not like fish, it is recommended that you take 0.5 to 1.8 grams of fish oil per day as supplements. That way you will get enough eicosapentaenoic acid (EPA) and docosahexaenoic acid (DHA).

Fish oil can help keep your heart healthy. But some experts also believe that fish oil is an important bipolar supplement and that it plays a key role in brain function and behavior. These experts report that omega-3 fatty acids may be helpful for those with bipolar disorder, particularly if they have an higher risk of cardiovascular disease or high triglycerides.

Some research suggests that getting more omega-3 fatty acids found in fish oil is linked to greater volume in areas of the brain. In particular, these areas are related to mood and behavior. Results from one study of 75 patients describe the benefits of omega-3 fatty acids compared to a placebo. The benefits included decreasing depression in bipolar disorder.

If you're a vegetarian or vegan looking for possible benefits of fish oil, go with nuts. Walnuts, flaxseed, and canola oil contain alpha-linolenic acid (ALA), which is converted to omega-3 fatty acid in the body.

Which Foods to Avoid for bi-polar sufferers

Some general dietary recommendations for treating bipolar disorder include:

- Getting only moderate amounts of caffeine and not stopping caffeine use abruptly
- Avoiding high-fat meals to lower the risk for obesity
- Watching your salt if you have high blood pressure but not skimping on salt if you are being prescribed lithium since low salt intake can cause higher levels of lithium in the blood
- Following your doctor's instructions to stay away from foods that may affect your specific bipolar medication, if any

In addition, you need to be wary of natural dietary supplements that can cause a drug-herb interaction.

Avoiding too much Caffeine may be helpful for getting good sleep, which is especially important for people with bipolar disorder. When someone with bipolar disorder is feeling depressed, extra caffeine can help that person boost the low mood. The problem is caffeine can disrupt sleep. Caffeine can also lower the sedative effects of medications, such as benzodiazepines, that are used to treat anxiety and mania associated with bipolar disorder.

In addition to lowering caffeine, it's important to avoid high-fat meals with some bipolar medications. High-fat meals may delay the time it takes for some bipolar medications to take effect. Talk to your doctor about your medications and necessary dietary changes.

If you take MAO inhibitors (a certain class of antidepressant that includes Emsam, Nardil, and Parnate), it's important to avoid tyramine-containing foods. These foods can cause severe hypertension in people taking MAO inhibitors. Some foods high in tyramine are:

- Overly ripe bananas and banana peels
- Tap beer
- Fermented cheese
- Aged meats
- Some wines, such as Chianti
- Soy sauce in high quantities

Your doctor can give you a list of foods to avoid if you take these drugs. Also, avoid taking natural dietary supplements if you are taking bipolar medications. Supplements such as St. John's wort and SAM-e are touted to treat moderate depression. A few studies show benefit for some people with depression. But these natural therapies can interact with antidepressants and other bipolar medications. Discuss any natural dietary supplement with your doctor to make sure it is safe.

What About Alcohol and Bipolar Disorder?

Instructions for most psychiatric medications warn users not to drink alcohol, but people with bipolar disorder frequently abuse alcohol and other drugs. The abuse is possibly an attempt to self-medicate or to treat their disturbing mood symptoms, and they may also cause mood symptoms that can mimic those of bipolar disorder.

Alcohol is a depressant. That is why many people use it as a tranquilizer at the end of a hard day or as an assist for tense social situations. While some patients stop drinking when they are depressed, it is more common that someone with bipolar disorder drinks during low moods. According to research, people with bipolar disorder are five times more likely to develop alcohol misuse and dependence than the rest of the population.

The link between bipolar disorder and substance abuse is explosive. Alcohol is a leading trigger of depressive episodes in many people who are genetically vulnerable for depression or bipolar disorder. About 15% of all adults who have a psychiatric illness in any given year also experience a co-occurring substance abuse disorder. This disorder can seriously complicate treatment.

Drinking grapefruit juice while on Bipolar drugs

Be careful. Talk to your doctor or pharmacist about eating grapefruit or drinking grapefruit juice with your bipolar medication. Grapefruit juice may increase the blood levels of certain bipolar medications. This includes some anticonvulsants. Taking benzodiazepines -- Klonopin, Xanax, Valium, Ativan -- with grapefruit juice may cause excessive impairment and even toxicity.

Should I take Bipolar medication with or without food?

Each bipolar medication is different. So talk with your doctor or pharmacist before taking the first dose. Some bipolar drugs can be taken with or without food. Others are less effective if taken with food. Your doctor or pharmacist will have the latest recommendations on taking the bipolar medication so you can safely take the medicine and get the full benefit of the drug.

In the next chapter we will be looking at rights in the workplace for those with bipolar disorder.

Now read the main points from Chapter 11 overleaf

****

Main points from Chapter 11

❖ Although there is no specific bipolar diet, nevertheless, it is very important indeed to make wise dietary choices that will help you maintain a healthy weight and stay well. This applies to all people, whether bi-polar sufferers or not.

❖ It is generally acknowledged that eating fatty fish at least two times a week is good for most people

❖ If you're a vegetarian or vegan looking for possible benefits of fish oil, go with nuts. Walnuts, flaxseed, and canola oil contain alpha-linolenic acid (ALA), which is converted to omega-3 fatty acid in the body.

❖ Some general dietary recommendations for treating bipolar disorder include getting only moderate amounts of caffeine and not stopping caffeine use abruptly, avoiding high-fat meals to lower the risk for obesity, watching your salt if you have high blood pressure but not skimping on salt if you are being prescribed lithium since low salt intake can cause higher levels of lithium in the blood and following your doctor's instructions to stay away from foods that may affect your specific bipolar medication, if any.

❖ Avoid taking natural dietary supplements if you are taking bipolar medications.

❖ The link between bipolar disorder and substance abuse is explosive. Alcohol is a leading trigger of depressive episodes in many people who are genetically vulnerable for depression or bipolar disorder.

12

Rights in the Workplace for Those with Bipolar Disorder

Rights of the employee who has bipolar disorder

Alongside stress, mental health problems are now the leading cause of absence from work. However, taking sick leave is no longer considered the best solution-for employees or employers. The chances of individuals returning to work after a prolonged leave of absence are slim. In recent years, there has been a move away from sick leave to a more optimistic plan of work based recovery.

Originally piloted in Wales and now rolled out throughout the UK, the governments fit-note programme sees work as a prescription towards recovery. The fit-note highlights areas of suitable employment in respect of an identified illness. The Fit note aims to encourage communication between doctor, patient and employer to help facilitate a return to work as soon as possible.

Working with bipolar

People with mental health problems generally experience prejudice, both in wider society and also in the workplace. This is largely down to ignorance. An employer has a duty to provide a working environment that encourages good mental health. They also have a duty to combat any damaging practices within the workplace, such as bullying. By educating staff about mental health, their preconceptions can be challenged.

Warning signs at work

Where you work and what you do will have an effect on you and will result in varying amounts of stress. As we have discussed earlier, stress is very much the enemy of a person suffering with bi-polar disorder. To maintain a healthy and productive working role it is important to feel that you have control over your work, as well as understanding the demands of your job.

The most common causes of work stress and mental health problems are increased work intensity, less security, less autonomy, target driven work cultures, which are increasing, and bullying and harassment. Look out for warning signs that your work is being affected by your condition. If you start to notice any of these warning signs then it is time to get some support. You need to talk to your manager or your HR department and they should work with you to make any changes needed. Avoiding the problem will make things worse, it is far better to deal with the issues sooner rather than later.

Examples of different warning signs

For those with bipolar, the following should alert you to the fact that something is wrong:

- Decreased concentration and memory
- Difficulties making a decision
- Nervousness and fear

- Sadness
- Headaches and chest pains
- Sleep disturbance and fatigue
- Being less agreeable with others
- Increased use of substances
- Repetitive thinking
- Negative thinking
- Frustration and irritability
- Weight fluctuation
- Taking risks with health

Medication

There may be times when you have to change your medication following advice from your GP or psychiatrist. It is therefore important that your employer understands this and allows for periods of absence whilst you adjust.

Self-management

We discussed self-management earlier in the book. Self-management is about recognising triggers of an episode of mania or depression and managing your lifestyle around them to avoid them. Some of the most common triggers are sleep deprivation, relationship problems and, in some cases, a reaction to excess amounts of caffeine, alcohol or cigarettes. The majority of these problems can be avoided if managed properly. For situations outside your control, it is important that safety nets are in place to avoid illness. For example, being allowed time off to attend outpatient appointments or counselling an help head off an episode of manic depression.

Support

An employee with bipolar disorder has a responsibility to know their personal management needs and to inform their employer about their condition. Correspondingly, it is the employer's responsibility to recognise that the individual is attempting to manage their illness and to put simple policies in place to prevent unnecessary stress or anxiety for all their employees. There is a clear framework of law which covers bi-polar disorder: The Health and safety at Work Act 1974, The Disability Discrimination Act 1995, as amended in 2005 and the Equality Act 2010.

The Health and Safety at Work Act 1974

Under this Act, all employers have a duty of reasonable care for their employees. This includes the mental well-being of an individual. Employers must assess all health and safety risks, take preventative action and carry out health and safety training in the workplace. The responsibility for monitoring these acts rests with the Health and Safety Executive (HSE). The HSE, in addition to assisting the employer, can also serve notices and set deadlines to encourage development in areas of safety.

The Disability Discrimination Act 1995 (DDA) as amended

The DDA provides protection to those with a disability It states " a person has a disability...if he has a physical or mental impairment which has a substantial and long term adverse effect on his ability to carry out normal day to day activities".

The DDA lists a number of disorders, including bi-polar disorder. The 2005 Act added that mental impairment need not be clinically recognised. The words "long term" mean likely to last 12 months or more. The DDA covers all employers regardless of size. It also protects agency staff and job applicants. There are a few exclusions to the Act:

- Members of the Armed Forces
- Those with addictions or dependence on substances not medically recognised
- Those with seasonal allergic rhinitis
- People who have tendencies to set fires, steal or abuse others
- People with conditions such as exhibitionism or voyeurism
- Those with tattoos and body piercing

Unlawful discrimination in employment

The DDA makes it unlawful for an employer at any establishment in Great Britain to discriminate against those with a disability in areas of applications for employment, promotion, training and development, terms and conditions benefits and the dismissal process. Needless to say, not all employers follow the law. One of the most difficult areas to prove is the application and interview process.

Definition of unlawful discrimination

Basically, discrimination occurs when a disabled person is treated less favourably than someone else.

Under the DDA, an employer can discriminate against a person in the following ways:

- Direct discrimination-by treating a disabled person less favourably on the grounds of disability. Examples include refusing to employ someone when they declare their disability or a blanket ban policy
- Disability related discrimination-by treating a disabled person less favourably for a reason related to their disability. One such example may be an employer dismissing an employee if they took extended sick leave due to a relapse of bi-polar
- By failing to make reasonable adjustments in the workplace or working arrangements
- Victimisation of a person (whether or not that person is disabled).

The Equality Act 2010

New ways of claiming disability discrimination have been introduced with the Equality Act. Direct discrimination and harassment based on association (an individual who is associated with a disabled person) or perception (an individual who looks as though they have a disability which they do not have) under the Equality Act is also unlawful.

The Government has published a code of practice, under the DDA, to provide practical guidance about the elimination of discrimination against disabled people in the field of employment. A code does not impose legal obligations, but industrial tribunals and courts must take account of the code, where relevant, when considering cases.

Return to work

If you have been on sick leave, it is very useful to arrange a return-to-work meeting to discuss your needs and your employer's expectations. You might find it useful to include your psychiatrist in the meeting. if this can be arranged. You can also request union representation if this is available. During this meeting, you should discuss and agree any adjustments that need to be made. Agree how progress will be monitored and what colleagues will be told. You should ask your employer to identify specific tasks and roles for your return and confirm a suitable return date. It is very important that you believe that you are ready to go back and engage positively in the workplace.

Access to work

This is a Department of Work and Pensions scheme designed to financially assist employers with costs beyond that of reasonable adjustments, helping to produce a more efficient support system in the workplace. Examples can include awareness training for staff, sickness cover for those with a fluctuating condition and any specialist equipment to assist in adapting to roles. You must be in employment to qualify for access to work. You should visit www.direct.gov.uk for more details.

In the next chapter we will be looking at welfare benefits available to those with bipolar disorder.

Now read the main points from Chapter 12 overleaf

****

Main points from Chapter 12

❖ Alongside stress, mental health problems are now the leading cause of absence from work. However, taking sick leave is no longer considered the best solution-for employees or employers.

❖ People with mental health problems generally experience prejudice, both in wider society and also in the workplace. This is largely down to ignorance. An employer has a duty to provide a working environment that encourages good mental health. They also have a duty to combat any damaging practices within the workplace, such as bullying. By educating staff about mental health, their preconceptions can be challenged.

❖ An employee with bipolar disorder has a responsibility to know their personal management needs and to inform their employer about their condition. Correspondingly, it is the employer's responsibility to recognise that the individual is attempting to manage their illness and to put simple policies in place to prevent unnecessary stress or anxiety for all their employees. There is a clear framework of law which covers bi-polar disorder: The Health and safety at Work Act 1974, The Disability Discrimination Act 1995, as amended in 2005 and the Equality Act 2010.

13

Welfare benefits available for those with Bipolar Disorder

The range of welfare benefits available

As someone with bipolar disorder, you will need to understand how the benefit system works and just what you may be entitled to if you are placed in a position where you are finding work difficult and you have to either work part time or give up work altogether. The summary below covers all benefits and makes reference to those that are particulalry pertinent to bipolar sufferers or to those with mental health problems generally. However, it is up to you to decide which benefit will apply to you, given your circumstances.

Checking your benefit entitlement

The Department for Work and Pensions (DWP) and your local council are not obliged to inform you which benefits you are entitled to, which means it is your responsibility to ensure you are claiming all of the relevant benefits.

If you are having problems with benefits then a welfare rights adviser may be able to help. This is someone that specialises in benefits. They can check that you are receiving everything you are entitled to, assist with claims and help with appeals if anything goes wrong. You can find a local adviser by contacting a local advice agency such as a Citizens Advice Bureau. If you have a support package as a bipolar sufferer then the person representing you will guide you towards an advisor.

Universal Credit (UC)

'Universal Credit' will replace the following benefits when it is rolled out in (initially, the aim was to roll out the new system in 2013 but there are currently delays):

- Income-based Job Seekers Allowance
- Income-related Employment and Support Allowance
- Income Support
- Tax Credits
- Housing Benefit

The Department for Work and Pensions (DWP) was planning for all new claimants to claim UC in October 2013, with existing benefits claimants being moved over to the new benefit by 2017. However, watch the press for up to date details.

You can claim UC if your household income is low and you don't have much in savings. You can qualify whether you are in or out of work. This is important to note if you are forced to work part time because of your condition.

Employment and Support Allowance (ESA)

ESA is a benefit you can claim if you are too unwell to work. It was introduced in 2008 for new claimants, and everyone who is currently claiming Incapacity Benefit, Income Support (on the grounds of disability) or Severe Disablement Allowance will be assessed using the ESA criteria sometime between 2011 and 2014.

In order to make a decision about your ability to work the Department for Work and Pensions (DWP) will carry out a 'Work Capability Assessment' (WCA). This involves you (or your representative) completing a form called the ESA50 and providing the DWP with supporting medical evidence. You will usually have to attend an independent medical assessment carried out by a heath care professional from an organisation called Atos.

ESA can either be contribution based or income related, the main difference between the two is that contribution based ESA is not affected by your savings or income or the income of other people in your household whereas income related ESA is. You automatically qualify for help with prescription charges when claiming income related ESA. You will be given the contribution based benefit if you have paid or been credited with sufficient national insurance (NI) contributions.

If you do not meet the NI contributions conditions you will have to apply for income related ESA which is means tested. This means the amount of benefit you receive will be affected by most other forms of income and any capital or savings worth £6000 or more. If you have capital or savings worth more than £16000 you will not receive any income related ESA.

From October 2013 (however, check dates as this seems to be moving back all the time) if you do not meet the NI contributions conditions you will have to apply for Universal

Credit on the grounds that you have limited capability for work, rather than income related ESA.

Job seekers allowance

JSA is a benefit for people who are unemployed and are available for full-time employment. If you are working less than 16 hours a week you can still claim JSA. Depending on your circumstances, you can sometimes keep up to £20 a week of earnings but you must be looking and available for full-time work.

JSA can either be contribution based or income related, the main difference between the two is that contribution based JSA is not affected by your savings or income or the income of other people in your household whereas income based JSA is. You automatically qualify for help with prescription charges when claiming income based JSA. You will be given the contribution based benefit if you have paid or been credited with sufficient national insurance (NI) contributions.

If you do not meet the NI contributions conditions you will have to apply for income based JSA which is means tested. This means the amount of benefit you receive will be affected by most other forms of income and any capital or savings worth £6000 or more. If you have capital or savings worth more than £16000 you will not receive any income based JSA.

Depending on where you live, during October 2013 if you do not meet the NI contributions conditions you will have to apply for Universal Credit rather than income based JSA. (Again, check dates)

When you apply for JSA you will be required to sign a jobseekers agreement, which is a contract that will be drawn up on the first interview, stating that you are actively seeking full-time employment and setting out what you are going to do in order to find work. When a job seekers agreement is set up it is important to think about any limitations your illness or disability may cause as these should be factored into the contract.

You will usually be asked to attend a meeting to 'sign on' every two weeks where you will have to show that you are fulfilling the jobseekers agreement by looking for work.

You can ask to speak to the Disability Employment Adviser (DEA) at your local Jobcentre Plus if you are claiming JSA and they could help you with your claim.

Income Support (IS)

You can claim income support if you are on a low income and not obliged to look for work because you are caring for someone or you are a lone parent of a child who is under five years old. There are other reasons that a person can claim Income Support but the rules are complex and cannot be covered in this summary. If you think you should be claiming Income support rather than ESA or JSA, it is recommended that you get assistance from a welfare rights adviser.

Incapacity Benefit (IB)

New claims for incapacity benefit stopped in October 2008 and were replaced by ESA. Some people are still receiving this benefit, but at the beginning of 2011 existing claimants of Incapacity

Benefit started being reassessed using the ESA rules. The reassessment process is expected to take until March 2014. Your claim will not be reviewed if you reach pension age before 6th April 2014.

It is difficult to say exactly when an existing claimant of Incapacity Benefit will be reassessed for ESA, but the Jobcentre Plus helpline may be able to provide an approximate time frame if they are aware that not knowing is causing you anxiety.

Severe Disablement Allowance (SDA)

New claims for SDA stopped in April 2001, but if you were already claiming this benefit at that time, your claim may have been allowed to continue. SDA, like Incapacity Benefit is now being replaced by Employment & Support Allowance. The DWP aim to have all existing IB & SDA claimants reassessed for ESA by 2014.

It is difficult to say exactly when your SDA will be reviewed, but the Jobcentre Plus helpline may be able to provide an approximate time frame if they are aware that not knowing is causing you anxiety. You will be contacted by the DWP when your claim is going to be reviewed. Your SDA claim will not be reviewed if you are going to reach pension age before 6th April 2014.

Statutory Sick Pay (SSP)

SSP is not a really a welfare benefit. It is paid by employers to employees who are unable to work due to sickness. Employers are under a legal obligation to pay SSP for a maximum of 28 weeks if you meet the criteria. SSP is paid at £86.70 per week, but some employers will pay more. This is called contractual sick pay. You should check your contract of employment to see what you will be paid in the event of sickness. When your SSP is due to end, your employer will send you a form called an SSP1. If you are still too unwell to work at the point when SSP stops, you should claim ESA.

Working Tax Credit

If you are in paid work but have a low income you may be able to claim Working Tax Credits (WTC) to top up your wages. WTC is administered by Her Majesty's Revenue & Customs (HMRC) who have a tax credit calculator on their website:

http://www.hmrc.gov.uk/taxcredits/payments-entitlement/entitlement/question-how-much.htm

You may be entitled to an additional amount of WTC called the disability element, if you are disabled and your disability affects your chances of obtaining work. To qualify for the disability element you must:

- Usually work more than 16 hours per week
- Be able to show that your disability puts you at a disadvantage of finding work
- Receive, or recently received, a qualifying benefit – these include Disability Living Allowance, Personal Independence Payment, Incapacity Benefit and Employment and Support Allowance among others

Examples of a person who is at a disadvantage of finding work due to a mental illness may be:

- Someone who is receiving treatment or under supervision of a mental health professional
- A person who is often confused or forgetful
- Someone who has difficulty forming normal social relationships

If you are employed but suffer a reduction in earnings due to reduced hours, or an SSP/ESA claim, your entitlement to Working Tax Credits may change and you could be able to claim more money. It is important to inform HMRC of any changes in income or number of working hours so they can adjust your payment accordingly.

Disability Living Allowance (DLA) and Personal Independence Payment (PIP)

Disability Living Allowance (DLA) is a benefit for people with disabilities who need help with their personal care and/or help getting around. It has two components: a care component, which could be paid at one of three rates (lower, middle and higher); and a mobility component which has two rates (lower and higher). If you have both care and mobility needs you may receive payment for both components

DLA can be paid on top of Income Support, Employment and Support Allowance, Jobseekers Allowance and other benefits and will not reduce the amount you get. In some cases getting an award of DLA can actually increase the amount you get in other benefits. You can claim DLA regardless of your employment status.

From 8th April 2013, a new benefit called the Personal Independence Payment (PIP) was introduced to replace DLA. Initially, only new claimants in selected parts of the North of England will need to claim PIP. However, the DWP is hoping that from July, all new claimants will claim PIP. Most existing DLA claimants with an indefinite award will not be affected until 2015 unless their circumstances changed after Oct 2013.

Housing Benefit

If you are on a low income and live in rented accommodation you may be able to claim Housing Benefit (HB) to help with the cost of rent. You can claim HB if you live in a property owned by a close relative as long as they do not live in the same household; however the rules can be complicated so it is recommended that you speak to a welfare rights adviser before claiming housing benefit for a property owned by a family member.

Council or housing association property

If your only income is from means tested benefits and you live in a property owned by the local authority or housing association your HB will usually cover the whole of your rent. If however you have additional income you may only get part of the rent paid, in which case you will be responsible for paying the shortfall. You may also have to top up your housing benefit if:

- Part of your rent pays for bills or services that are not covered by HB (such as electricity, meals or laundry services)

- You have a non-dependant living with you (a non-dependant may be an adult child, friend or relative who will be expected to contribute towards the rent)

You may also have your housing benefit reduced if you have more bedrooms in your property than the government thinks that you need. This has, unofficially, been called the 'bedroom tax'

If you are under-occupying one bedroom then your housing benefit will be reduced by 14%. If you are under-occupying more than one bedroom, your housing benefit will be reduced by 25%.

You will not be regarded as under-occupying one of your bedrooms if you need that extra bedroom for a carer to stay overnight to provide care for you. A carer would actually have to do this regularly in order for you to claim the exemption. It is not necessary for you to claim DLA or PIP in order to show that you need a carer to provide this care as long as you have other evidence.

If you are affected by the 'bedroom tax', you have the following options:

- Move House
- Take in a lodger
- Apply for 'discretionary housing payments' from your local council
- Increase your hours of work
- Get a benefits check to make sure you are receiving everything you are entitled to

- Pay the difference out of your benefits or other income if you can afford to do this

Local Housing Allowance (LHA)

If you live in a property or room that is rented from a private landlord Local Housing Allowance rules are used to work out how much housing benefit you get. The LHA rates depend on where you live, the number of people in your household and the size of your accommodation. This can range from a single room in a shared house to a property with four bedrooms.

Changes to housing benefit regulations in April 2011 means the local housing allowance size criteria can be increased for a person who has an established need for overnight care, is actually receiving that care, and has an additional room in their property. This means that you may be able to claim housing benefit for a property with an additional room if you have a non-resident carer that regularly needs to stay overnight.

From January 1st 2012 people under 35 have had their benefit restricted to the shared room rate. However some people will not be affected by the changes. The rules will not apply to you if:

- You get the middle or higher rate care component of Disability Living Allowance and no-one receives Carer's Allowance for you.
- You live with someone else (for example, a partner, child, elderly relative, friend or grown-up child); who is part of your household.
- You rent from a Local Authority or housing association.
- You live in supported housing provided by a housing association, registered charity or voluntary organisation

and get a package of care or support from your landlord (or from somebody else on behalf of your landlord).

- Your private tenancy began before January 1989.

- You need an extra bedroom for a carer who does not live with you but who provides you with overnight care.

- You are under 22 and have been in the care of a local authority since the age of 16, or have been accommodated by a local authority since the age of 16.

- You have lived in a hostel for homeless people or a hostel that provides rehabilitation and resettlement within the community for at least three months. You must have received resettlement support to help you live in the community.

Support for Mortgage Interest (SMI)

If you live in a mortgaged property and you are claiming either income based ESA, Income Support or income based Jobseekers Allowance, you may be entitled to help with your mortgage payments through a benefit called Support for Mortgage Interest (SMI).

There is a 13 week waiting period from the time you claim until you get your first payment and payments will usually be made directly to your mortgage lender. SMI will only help with the interest portion of a mortgage up to the value of £200,000; it will not help pay back the amount you borrowed. The rate that SMI is paid at is based on the Bank of England's standard interest rate. You can find out how much the rate is at any time by checking 'support for mortgage interest' webpage at www.gov.uk.

If you do not have an interest-only mortgage you will either have to make up the shortfall on the actual mortgage payments to ensure you do not go into arrears, or come to a satisfactory arrangement with your lender such as switching to an interest-only mortgage. To apply for this benefit or to ask further questions you should contact Jobcentre Plus or the Pension Service. Their contact details are at the end of this section. When Universal Credit is introduced, it will include additional payments to meet mortgage interest costs.

Council Tax Support and Discounts

If you are liable for council tax and on a low income then you may be entitled to help with your council tax through Council Tax Support. This scheme replaced the national Council Tax Benefit on 1st April 2013. Council Tax Support is administered by your local authority through their local scheme, and may cover either part or your entire council tax bill depending on your household income. How much help you can get with your council tax will depend on your local scheme. However, the government has reduced the money available to local authorities by 10% and so it is likely that many working age people will have to contribute towards their council tax in order to make up the difference. It is important to ensure that your council tax bill is correct. If you are living alone or you are very unwell, you may be able to get your bill reduced.

Single person's discount

If you are the only adult living in a property you should be receiving a 'single person's discount' on your council tax bill, this will reduce the bill by 25%. You will also receive this discount if you are not the only adult, but the other people you live with are not liable to pay council tax because, for example they are students or exempt due to a 'severe mental impairment'.

Exemption due to severe mental impairment

The council tax rules say that a person is exempt from council tax if they have a 'severe mental impairment'. It states that 'a person is severely mentally impaired if he has a severe impairment of intelligence and social functioning (however caused) which appears to be permanent'.

To qualify for the exemption you must obtain confirmation from a doctor stating that you are severely mentally impaired and receive one of the following benefits:

- DLA with the middle or highest rate care component
- Personal Independence Payment Daily Living Component (standard or enhanced rate)
- Attendance Allowance
- Severe Disablement Allowance
- Employment and Support Allowance
- Incapacity Benefit
- Income Support or Jobseekers Allowance with a disability premium
- Working Tax Credit with the disability element

Disabled band reduction scheme

If you or a person that lives with you has a disability that means they require additional space, it may be possible to get the council tax bill reduced to the price of the next band down. So if, for example your property is in band C, you would be charged the band B rate.

To qualify for the disabled band reduction you would have to show that the property is the main residence of at least one disabled person. The property must also have an additional room to meet the needs of the disabled person (if the room is not a kitchen or bathroom it must be for the predominant use of the disabled person); or additional space to allow for wheelchair use.

If you think you should qualify for a band reduction, you should contact the local authority that issues your council tax bill.

The Social Fund

From April 2013, the discretionary social fund was disbanded. 'Crisis loans' and 'community care grants' will no longer be available. 'Budgeting loans' will continue to be available until they are replaced by 'budgeting advances' under the new Universal Credit scheme.

Crisis loans used to be very helpful to people who were experiencing a delay in the payment of their benefits for some reason. To replace crisis loans, the DWP can now provide 'short-term advances' to provide you with some money if you're having to wait for your benefits to be paid. The short-term advance will have to be paid back, just like a crisis loan.

Local authorities have been given the discretion to set up schemes to replace 'community care grants' if they would like to. Some local authorities may not set up schemes at all, and the ones that do may choose to do things very differently. We hope to be able to provide more information about this when we find out more about what local authorities are doing.

Now read the main points from Chapter 13 overleaf

****

Main points from chapter 13

❖ As someone with bipolar disorder, you will need to understand how the benefit system works and just what you may be entitled to if you are placed in a position where you are finding work difficult and you have to either work part time or give up work altogether.

❖ The Department for Work and Pensions (DWP) and your local council are not obliged to inform you which benefits you are entitled to, which means it is your responsibility to ensure you are claiming all of the relevant benefits.

❖ If you are having problems with benefits then a welfare rights adviser may be able to help. This is someone that specialises in benefits. They can check that you are receiving everything you are entitled to, assist with claims and help with appeals if anything goes wrong. You can find a local adviser by contacting a local advice agency such as a Citizens Advice Bureau. If you have a support package as a bi-polar sufferer then the person representing you will guide you towards an advisor.

Conclusion

Hopefully, this wide ranging book has touched on most of the areas of concern of those who have bipolar disorder. At the beginning, we described bipolar generally and then throughout the book we discussed the many aspects of the disorder that need to be understood, such as support and medication, the role of the GP and psychiatric profession and also the benefits of cognitive behavioural therapy.

Areas such as the family and welfare benefits, plus the rights of the employee in the workplace have also been covered.

My own personal experience of bipolar disorder has been through friends and I have seen at first-hand how this can affect people's lives and lead to a downward spiral. I have suffered with those people.

The outcome of my experience is this book, which I sincerely hope will go a long way to promoting an understanding of the condition and also help the reader raise his or her awareness of what they can do to alleviate the problems associated with bipolar.

Doreen Jarrett.

Useful addresses and Websites

Mental Health Act Commission
Maid Marion House
56 Houndsgate
Nottingham NG1 6BG
Tel: O115 943 7100
Internet: www.mhac.trent.nhs.uk

National Association of Citizens Advice Bureau
Central Office
Myddelton House
115-123 Pentonville Road
London N1 9LZ
Tel: 020 7833 2181
Internet: www.nacab.org.uk

Self-help organisations
Britain

Depression Alliance
35 Westminster Bridge Road
London SE1 7JB
Tel: 020 7633 0557
Fax: 020 7633 0559

Manic Depressive Fellowship National Office
Castleworks
21 St George's Road
London SE1 6ES
Tel: 020 7793 2600
Email: md@mdf.org.uk

Mental Health Foundation: UK Office
20-21 Corwall Terrace
London NW1 4QL
Tel:020 7535 7400
Email: mhf@mentalhealth.org.uk

MIND (The National Association for Mental Health)
15-19 Broadway
London E15 4BQ
Tel: 020 8519 2122
Fax: 020 8522 1725
Email: contact@mind.org.uk

Mood Swings Network
23 Mount Street
Manchester M4 4DE
Tel: 0161 953 4105

Bipolar UK National Office
11 Belgrave Road
London SW1V 1RB
Tel: 020 7931 6480
Fax: 020 7931 6481
Email: info@bipolaruk.org.uk
www.bipolaruk.org.uk

Bipolar UK
Clarence House
Clarence Place
Newport NP19 7AA
Email: walesinfo@bipolaruk.org.uk

Bipolar UK Member Services

To join please call us on Tel: 020 7931 6480

If you subscribe to member services you can call a dedicated helpline to assist with one off immediate needs.

For enquiries in the Midlands and North of England- and for all enquiries relating to self-help groups and employment please contact:

Midlands and the North of England Office

Bipolar UK

2 Macon Court

Herald Drive

Crewe

Cheshire CW1 6EA

Tel: 0845 434 9970 or 01270 230260

Email: groupdevelopment@bipolaruk.org.uk

Self-help websites for bipolar & depression-

www.depressionalliance.org

Above site for depression alliance which provides information on UK self-help groups as well as email contacts and chat rooms on bipolar disorder and depression more generally.

www.bipolarworld.net

An American information and support site for people with bipolar disorder, run mainly by service users. Includes chat rooms and internet-search service for bipolar-related topics.

www.mcmanweb.com

An American site run by someone with a diagnosis of bipolar disorder, who previously worked as a financial journalist. It provides information and updates on clinical research into bipolar disorder, as well as input from other service users and a discussion forum.

www.mdf.org.uk
A British site for the Manic Depressive Fellowship (address above) , which provides information on local self-help groups in the UK, contact information for MDF and listings of current MDF publications.

www.mentalhealth.org.uk
This Mental Health Foundation website covers mental-health issues relating to children and adults. It also funds research into these areas, and provides information on this. A number of the initiatives being developed by the Mental Health Foundation are described here, including their development of services with a significant amount of user involvement.

www.mind.org.uk
The British site for MIND (address above). A broad-ranging site covering self-help information, information on local MIND groups and email contacts. This site also provides information on current MIND campaigns and projects and opportunities within the organisation for voluntary and paid employment.

www.ndmda.org
An American site, providing educational information and support for people with bipolar disorder and depression.

www.pendulum.org
Another American site, providing information on recent developments in bipolar disorder. Books relevant to bipolar

disorder are listed and recent, usually American, research is highlighted. Informal jokes – and fun-pages are included. The site has a bipolar-focused search engine.

www.windsofchange.com
A Canadian site, providing information on topics relevant to people with bipolar disorder and their carers. Again, there is a forum on site for users and carers.
Bipolar and Pregnancy
Where can I learn more or find support?

Action on Postpartum Psychosis (APP) is a charity run by a group of women who have suffered with this illness, clinicians and academic researchers. They have a website to provide support and information for other women in a similar position and their partners: www.app-network.org

APP would also be interested to hear from women with bipolar who are pregnant or considering pregnancy, so they can keep them informed of research projects which might interest them. You can join for free and receive occasional emails about the latest news and research. The website also contains advice on recovery, personal stories and details of a Peer Support Network using trained volunteers who have recovered from postpartum psychosis themselves.

Bipolar UK the national charity for people affected by bipolar including families, carers and loved ones. They provide a range of services across England and Wales including self help groups and regularly run workshops at their Annual Conference on the issues facing women who have bipolar and want to start a family. See: www.bipolaruk.org.uk

There is also a thread on the charity's web-based forum – the eCommunity – accessed via the website, where these issues are discussed and women can support each other.

Other useful websites:

The Royal College of Psychiatrists (www.rcpsych.ac.uk)
This site has excellent leaflets on postnatal depression and postpartum psychosis.

Postpartum Support International – PSI (www.postpartum.net)
An international network that links volunteers, support groups, and professionals, particularly strong in the US.

PNI ORG UK (Post Natal Illness) (www.pni.org.uk)
An information sitye for sufferers and survivors of all types of postnatal illness.

Bipolar Disorder Research Network (www.bdrn.org)
BDRN is a group of researchers and research participants in the UK undertaking a major study investigating the underlying causes of bipolar disorder.

BEPCymru (www.bep-c.org)
A group education programme featuring an excellent video aimed at people with bipolar disorder considering pregnancy.

Association for Postnatal illness (www.apni.org)
Helpline: 020 7386 0868. Provides a telephone helpline, information leaflets and a network of volunteers who have themselves experienced PND.

Cry-sis   (www.cry-sis.org.uk)
Helpline: 08451 228 669. Provides self-help and support for families with excessively crying and sleepless and demanding babies.

Family Action (www.family-action.org.uk)
Tel: 020 7254 6251. Support and practical help for families affected by mental illness, including 'Newpin' services – offering support to parents of children under-5 whose mental health is affecting their ability to provide safe parenting.

Home Start (www.home-start.org.uk)
Tel: 0800 068 6368. Support and practical help for families with at least one child under-5. Help offered to parents finding it hard to cope for many reasons. These include PND or other mental illness, isolation, bereavement, illness of parent or child.

Meet-Mum-Association (MAMA) (www.mama.co.uk)
Helpline: 0845 120 3746. Support and information for all mums and mums-to-be who are lonely, isolated or depressed in pregnancy or after having a baby. Local groups and on-line support.

Netmums (www.netmums.com/pnd)
A website offering support and information on pregnancy and parenting. There is also information on local resources and support groups.

The Samaritans (www.samaritans.org)
24-hour helpline 08457 90 90 90 (UK) or 1850 60 90 90 (Ire); Email:jo@samaritans.org

Index

Access to work, 111
Aggressive behaviour, 13
Aggressiveness, 7, 78
Amitriptyline, 40
Anger, 72, 73, 76
Anticonvulsant drugs, 6, 38
Anti-depressants, 6, 39
Anti-parkinsonian drugs, 6, 42
Antipsychotic drugs, 41
Appetit, 15
Assertiveness, 7, 77, 78

Behavioural therapy, 6, 54
Bipolar 1 disorder, 15
Bipolar 2 disorder, 16
Breathing Exercise, 69

Caffeine, 85, 99
Carbamazepine, 38, 39
Care co-ordinators, 50
Care Programme Approach (CPA), 49
Child and Adolescent Mental Health Service (CAMHS), 45, 52
Childhood bi-polar disorder, 18
Childhood distress, 5, 17
Cognitive behavioral therapy, 49
Cognitive therapy, 6, 53, 54
Community mental health teams, 6, 48
Community psychiatric nurse, 49
Council Tax Support, 125
Cyclothymia, 16

Delayed sleep phase syndrome, 83
Delusions, 12
Department for Work and Pensions (DWP, 113, 114, 115, 129
Depression, 5, 12, 14, 16, 62, 133

Diet, 5, 30, 97
Dietary supplements, 100
Disability Living Allowance (DLA, 120

Employment and Support Allowance (ESA), 114
Equality Act 2010, 9, 108, 110, 112

Family Issues, 8, 91
Family therapy, 50
Fatigue, 15
Fish Oil, 98

Grapefruit Juice, 101
Grief, 17, 92, 95
Group therapy, 50

Health and Safety at Work Act 1974, 8, 108
Her Majesty's Revenue & Customs (HMRC, 119
Hospitalization, 51
Housing Benefit, 114, 121
Hypomania, 5, 12, 14

Income Support, 114, 117, 120, 124, 126
Income-based Job Seekers Allowance, 114
Income-related Employment and Support Allowance, 114
Insomnia, 83
Irregular sleep-wake schedules, 83
Irritability, 15

Job seekers allowance, 9, 116

Lamotrigine, 38, 39
Largacti, 41
Lithium, 6, 37
Lithium carbonate, 37
Lithium Citrate, 37

Local Housing Allowance (LHA), 123

Managing bipolar disorder, 25
Manic episodes, 5, 13
Medication, 6, 8, 35, 37, 101, 107
Minor tranquillisers, 42
Mixed episodes, 12
Mortgage Interest, 124

National Institute for Health and Care Excellence (NICE, 35, 44
Neuroleptics, 41
Non-Assertiveness, 77

Omega 3, 31

Parental support, 91
Parkinson's, 16, 24
Personal Independence Payment (PIP), 120, 121
Pregnancy, 20, 137
Progressive Muscle Relaxation, 70
Prozac, 40
Psychodynamic therapists, 6, 50
Psychoeducation, 49
Psychotherapy, 49

Relaxation, 7, 30, 68, 70
Relaxation techniques, 30
REM (rapid eye movement, 83, 89
Return to work, 111
Rights in the Workplace, 105
Risky behaviour, 13

Sadness, 107
Self-management, 8, 107
Seroxat, 40
Shame, 7, 61

Single person's discount, 125
Sleep disturbance, 17, 107
Social Fund, 127
Sodium valproate, 38
Spouses, 92, 95
Statutory Sick Pay (SSP), 118
Stigma, 7, 61, 62
Stigmatisation, 61, 66
Stress, 5, 27, 30, 68, 76, 86
Suicide, 15
Suppressing Anger, 73

Tax Credits, 114, 119, 120
The Disability Discrimination Act 1995 (DDA) as amended, 108
Trcyclic anti-depressants, 39

Universal Credit (UC), 114

Vicious cycles, 7, 67, 68, 76
Visualization, 71

Weight fluctuation, 107
Welfare benefits, 113
Working Tax Credit, 119, 126
Working with bipolar, 8, 105